EVOLVE

EVOLVE

The Business Partnering *Playbook*

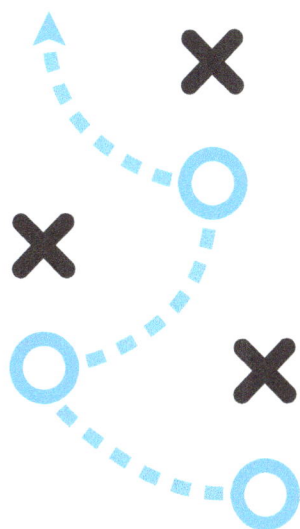

RITA CINCOTTA

GEORGE LIBEROPOULOS

Published by Rita Cincotta and George Liberopoulos

First published in 2021 in Melbourne, Australia

Copyright © Rita Cincotta and George Liberopoulos

www.impactology.com.au
www.ritacincotta.com

Melbourne, Victoria

The moral rights of the authors have been asserted.

Edited by Jenny Magee

Typeset and printed in Australia by BookPOD

ISBN: 978-0-6452963-0-3 (pbk)
eISBN: 978-0-6452963-1-0 (ebook)

Contents

Introduction

Business Partners are increasingly an integral part of organisations, partnering with business leaders as trusted confidants and bringing deep technical expertise without being limited by it. Neither stepping ahead nor falling behind; they are completely integrated into teams.

With increasing popularity and impact, the Business Partner role has become essential across many significant business functions, including finance, human resources, information technology, legal, risk and compliance, procurement, and marketing.

Since its inception, the role has evolved from assistance and advice to true partnering and collaboration. Once the focus on support meant limited accountability for outcomes, now decisions, initiatives and outcomes are shared with leaders and their teams.

We are inspired by the great work of David Ulrich at the University of Michigan and The RBL Group. He has pioneered the direction of the HR profession and the HR Business Partnering role for more than three decades. Ulrich's commitment to research with his collaborators, including Wayne Brockbank and others, has had a profound impact on the field of HR.

In their 2005 book, *The HR Value Proposition*, Ulrich and Brockbank posed a series of future-focused questions to sharpen and enhance the value of HR. These questions included: 'How do we create a powerful line of sight between business strategy and HR?' 'How does HR help to build, not just measure, intangible value creation?' and 'How do we develop more capable HR professionals and departments to do all this?' (Ulrich & Brockbank, 2005).

We reframe these questions and ask, 'How do we create a powerful line of sight between business strategy and Business Partners regardless of discipline?' 'How do Business Partners collaboratively help build, not just measure, intangible value creation?' and 'How do we develop the capability of Business Partners to do this?'

> As there is no formal education path for a Business Partner, skills are built based on what others see and do and through lived experience.

The Business Partner role is now about partnerships more than ever, but the capabilities required for development and progression to develop skills to build quality and sustainable partnerships haven't always kept up with the speed of change. As there is no formal education path for a Business Partner, skills are built based on what others see and do and through lived experience. While practical, this can make for an inconsistent service proposition.

Having led various teams, including Business Partners for more than a decade, we, Rita and George, have spent the past three years focused on what business partnering is and isn't – and what it can be moving forward. We understand what makes a great Business Partner and what it takes to create a service model that best supports them, so they, in turn, can best back their clients. We've also expanded that line of sight to understand better how business partners from all disciplines can collaborate and deliver greater value for the organisation. A re-imagined version of Aristotle's famous quote could read: 'The whole of business partnering is greater than the sum of its parts.'

Rita's story

When I started my HR career more than twenty years ago, Business Partner seemed like the ultimate role. I admired their ability to be closely connected with the business while being such impressive technical experts, and I could see that Business Leaders valued them as team members. I observed with interest, so I could emulate what I was seeing. The connection between the Business Partners and Business Leaders provided insight into the value of the role to the business. It also guided my development around business and success measures

> The connection between the Business Partners and Business Leaders provided insight into the value of the role to the business.

and gave my commercial acumen far greater lift than any post graduate qualification.

When leading teams of Business Partners, I became more interested in service models and the client experience in accessing my team's services, wanting to ensure the service was accessible, responsive and of high quality. I focused on the consistency of the experience of different clients and Business Partners, ensuring that senior Business Partners could share their insights and experiences with junior Business Partners.

Decades on, I realise that businesses have many more Business Partners than are acknowledged in their organisational chart, even at the C-suite level.

George's story

My first Business Partner role was also more than twenty years ago, and I remember how daunting it was to have leaders turn to me for advice and support. I was neither effective nor efficient! But what I lacked in capability, I made up for in willingness to listen to feedback. One of my mentors always says, 'Feedback is a gift', and this gift has continued to feed my curiosity and willingness to learn and develop. Having worked as a Business Partner across multiple disciplines and levels of seniority, I recognise a common thread, a consistent language of what it means to deliver greater value and impact to the business. At the core of this book is the need to empower all Business Partners – to articulate the behavioural attributes required for business partnering success and improve the commercial acumen of Business Partners to help drive deeper and more meaningful problem-solving conversations. Let's focus on breaking down the real and perceived barriers that prevent effective relationships within your discipline area and with your business partnering colleagues.

Who is this book for?

We've written this for current and aspiring Business Partners who provide internal consulting roles in organisations as part of an enabling function. Our purpose is to highlight the need for ongoing review and evolution of the Business Partner role in generating better business outcomes. Without change and growth, Business Partners risk remaining locked in what they know and negatively impact business leaders' views of the role.

We've interviewed, coached, and developed hundreds of Business Leaders and Business Partners whose insights contributed significantly to our understanding. We explored the most significant recent changes for Business Partners, considered what new skills or competencies Business Partners needed to

> Having worked as a Business Partner across multiple disciplines and levels of seniority, I recognise a common thread, a consistent language of what it means to deliver greater value and impact to the business.

develop, and recognised which capabilities are increasingly essential and define success. We have included many insights and quotes from our programs, interviews, and coaching sessions with several hundred Business Partners over three years.

> Fundamentally, work has changed forever in a post-pandemic world. There is no going back.

Fundamentally, work has changed forever in a post-pandemic world. There is no going back. Organisations are grappling with decisions that will best position their workforce for future success and wondering how employees can apply the skills they have built working differently. Specifically, they want Business Partners to be more progressive in their leadership style and contribution, given that the way we work, our systems, rhythms and processes have changed.

While the Business Partner role requirements vary considerably between organisations, technical domains, and industries, one aspect remains consistent: core capabilities elevate the quality of the Business Partner and the business' experience with them. How do we better equip Business Partners to adapt and boost the partnership experience and drive increased business value in a fast-changing environment?

What can you expect from reading this book?

Most importantly, you can expect to elevate your impact as a Business Partner.

Across six chapters, we will take you through the evolution of the Business Partnering role. Many call themselves Business Partners, but across different organisations, the role can be very different. We aim to provide a consistent understanding of the role, applicable across industries and geographies.

> We aim to provide a consistent understanding of the role, applicable across industries and geographies.

Chapter One opens the evolution of the role as we know it and what the future will require. The position stems from various disciplines and has different titles, and we look at how it is received and utilised in organisations.

Chapter Two considers how complexities in service models and systems can make business partnering more challenging.

Chapter Three introduces a value model that supports the evolution of the Business Partner and an impact model that represents the balance of relevant behavioural attributes and commercial acumen. Both of which improve the business partnering experience and drive superior business value. We unpack these in detail so you can assess where you may be on your business partnering journey and the development gaps you may need to fill.

Chapter Four considers the developing relationship between Business Partners and Business Leaders while building trust and value. We examine these from both perspectives, as while their issues may be similar, the variance is a valuable point of interest.

> Recent pressures require Business Partners to lead and manage change while adapting and developing resilience at an individual and organisational level.

Chapter Five introduces the Business Partnering Impact model. Our research has enabled us to find the right combination of competencies for the Business Partner role that apply across any area of technical expertise.

Chapter Six looks at the impact of change on the role, particularly given the global pandemic. Recent pressures require Business Partners to lead and manage change while adapting and developing resilience at an individual and organisational level.

Each chapter concludes with key highlights and questions for your reflection.

Throughout the book, we will share ways to elevate the experience for your clients and inspire increased business value. These key outcomes are driven through the Business Partnering Impact model.

PART ONE

Background and Context

CHAPTER ONE

- - - - - - - - - - - - - -

The Role of the Business Partner

Frequent change and disruption, market uncertainties and rapid innovation are some of the many factors impacting businesses today. Expectations of the Business Partner have evolved considerably in recent years, and with these heightened expectations comes the need to refresh and upskill to keep up with increased business demands.

Now more than ever, we live in a volatile, uncertain, complex, and ambiguous world. Represented by the acronym VUCA, the term was first coined in the 1980s by Warren Bennis and Burt Nanus, highlighting the unpredictability of our modern world (Bennis, 1986). It is even more relevant as we come through the COVID pandemic as Business Partners must be ahead of the challenges this fast-changing environment presents. They need to bring insight that sits ahead of any impacts felt by the ever-increasing business complexity. This requires strategic foresight, a strong knowledge of the business and the environment in which it operates. One Business Partner in the fast-moving consumer goods (FMCG) industry commented, 'Until you prove yourself at that strategic level, you won't get the chance to perform at that level'. Trust and credibility are integral to the businesspartnering role.

Definition of business partnering

What do we mean by the term business partnering?

Historically it refers to the role of internal consultants or advisors in enabling functions in an organisational operating model. Simply put, they support a business to succeed.

Business Partners appear in organisations of varying sizes, industries, and complexity. They can have different titles and sit at different levels, making it challenging to understand the role broadly. The role has become ubiquitous in recent years, with Business Partners appearing across many disciplines and effectively supporting leaders and their teams in specific business areas. This support can be varied and often depends on the Business Partner's capability and the leader's willingness to integrate them into the business unit. A Business Partner usually has a home team that they belong to, for example, Finance or Human Resources, and they will also be a part of the leaders' groups they serve, such as the CFO, CIO, or HR

> Effective business partnering signifies positive action, a positive attitude to collaboration and problem-solving.

Director. We're exploring the concept of Business Partnering as a verb, not a noun. Effective business partnering signifies positive action, a positive attitude to collaboration and problem-solving. To enhance our understanding of the business partnering term, we're using the term Business Partner to develop an accurate current state and a proposed future state.

Evolution of the role

In earlier decades, the role was more transactional and operational, and, in the early 2000s, it appeared most often within the Human Resources profession. It emerged from a specific area of expertise (e.g. HR, both generalist and specialist areas) and partnered with another business area (e.g. sales, legal, or operations). The role required the Business Partner to focus specifically on the sector they supported. Since the 1990s, the role has evolved and is now found across most business disciplines.

The role has continued to evolve, particularly in recent times, from its beginnings as a technical advisor in an area of expertise to a broader business advisor that is an integral part of a leader's team.

In earlier times, the Business Partner would meet business needs such as producing reports, responding to operational enquiries, attending meetings, delivering training, and assisting with processes and systems. They have, and continue to be, the conduit between the department they support and the department they represent.

Now the role is evolving even further as Business Partners have greater integration and alignment with the work of the business.

They understand what drives revenue, what shareholders and clients want, and have an in-depth understanding of business strategy. This makes their value proposition as Business Partners far more holistic, as with a complete perspective, they can advise on commercial matters that span the whole business.

While the Business Partner's role has changed, their acceptance by a leader depends on several factors. Some leaders view the role through their personal experience and that of those who have previously supported them. And some may see it as superfluous or unnecessary, while others will be accustomed to working with a Business Partner.

> The Business Partner's service delivery is likely to be guided by client needs and strategy and play a role in identifying insights and trends.

The Business Partner's service delivery is likely to be guided by client needs and strategy and play a role in identifying insights and trends. Being part of the business unit they support and having an enabling function offers a perspective that looks up and out, rather than just in.

You cannot enrol in a Business Partner degree (yet). People come into the role from different backgrounds, academic studies and relative experience, although it does tend to evolve from others such as financial analyst, IT client manager, HR advisor, marketing consultant, risk advisor and procurement specialist. The move into a Business Partner role is usually a progression through a technical discipline (depth of expertise) that culminates in client contact and enough trust and credibility to represent the business area (breadth of expertise) confidently.

The service provided by the Business Partner

What makes a great Business Partner? It's a simple question that is challenging to answer. Business Partners come to the role with varying levels of technical and industry experience. They may have capability across more than one domain, such as people, operations, finance, and technology. Their experience, time spent in various industries, and past relationships with clients will positively or negatively impact their perceived value.

The service proposition for the role of a Business Partner will also be guided by what the internal client needs to deliver on business goals, which may vary from leader to leader within an organisation. A focus on service will ensure that the needs are reviewed regularly and that the internal client has what they need to undertake their work for the benefit of the business. We recommend at least annual reviews, with a framework for the service to be measured and valued.

Building relationships

Trust is central to the business partnering relationship, and throughout the book, we will explore how it can be developed and maintained.

In some businesses, the Business Partner role is clearly defined; however, it extends to many responsibilities in the enabling function. For example, the Chief Financial Officer and the Chief People Officer partner with the Chief Executive Officer and the Board in guiding the direction of the business. In these roles, they are partnering with other business leaders to lead and run the business effectively. Excellent Business Partners and Advisors often support great leaders. You become the trusted partner for the leader you are supporting.

Business relationships are critical. They enable us to get things done in an organisation. Beyond what we know, whom we know and how we build relationships and interact with colleagues helps build trust, rapport and credibility. Once a connection is sufficiently established, it provides the opportunity to become a trusted partner – vital for those in the business partnering role.

To change mindsets, the Business Partner must demonstrate their value proposition at a higher level and be responsive and patient as they build their offer. They need to articulate how this is integral to the business and the leaders they serve. At the same time, the Business Partner must meet the needs of their internal client.

The capability of the Business Partner

Ultimately the service provided by the Business Partner will depend on their capability, and this will hinge on several factors:

▶ Experience, including the level of leaders and clients they have worked with

▶ Knowledge beyond their area of expertise, representing the balance between breadth and depth of knowledge

▶ Understanding of the business and the industry

▶ The ability to build trusting relationships and influence stakeholders at all levels.

While the Business Partner may have acquired their expertise from various industries, experiences and even business disciplines, what qualifies them is their expertise and the ability to apply best-fit solutions to a business and build strong professional relationships. The capability of the Business Partner is also dependent on what they know (expertise and knowledge), how they communicate this expertise and knowledge and the growth that occurs through sharing and learning from others.

To be relevant and of service to their clients, a Business Partner needs to be constantly learning. The following model depicts the connection between expertise,

> To be relevant and of service to their clients, a Business Partner needs to be constantly learning.

communicating this expertise and their growth (and those they support). It emphasises that while the Business Partner is in a position of knowledge and providing advice, they learn as much as they may impart.

The Business Partner's capability can deepen through the application of the model. To take this further, when we communicate our expertise, we sit in the role of what Fred Kofman described as the knower, or the knowledge holder, sharing and imparting the knowledge. When we are the learner, we are open and curious. We ask and tell – rather than merely tell (Fred Kofman, author and a leadership and culture expert, 2006). From this, our expertise grows, and we provide a deeper understanding to the leaders we support. As a result, our service has a more significant impact. The model explores the symbiotic relationship of Expertise (what we know), Communication (how we communicate what we know) and Growth (how we grow by sharing what we know).

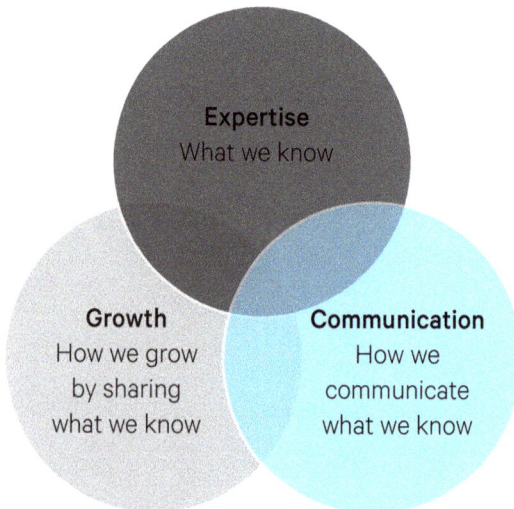

Figure 1: © The impact of growth, expertise and communication

Expertise

What we recognise as the skill of business partnership is gathered through a wide net of experience, qualifications, technical expertise in a business discipline, and experience in the type of business we support. Our expertise is our value currency.

We trade that expertise for validation, contribution, the opportunity to collaborate and the feeling of belonging received through this contribution and collaboration. How much our expertise is valued depends on how we package it. Are we easy to buy? Do we exhibit behaviours that are conducive to a productive and easy relationship with our clients? Is what we know relevant and current? We can have great expertise, but if our delivery compromises the value of the expertise, it becomes less relevant.

> The way we communicate what we know determines whether we are easy to work with.

Communication

The way we communicate what we know determines whether we are easy to work with. Our message delivery links to our ability to build relationships and be seen as trusted advisors (Maister, Green, & Galford, 2001). Listening well and clearly communicating ideas is vital. Maister describes this as earning the right to listen and comment. Do we have enough credibility, and have we built enough rapport to ensure that we will be heard and listen well? Are our ideas and input easily shared and understood? Do we communicate our expertise in a way that is easy for people to understand? What an individual will perceive as effective communication is subjective. Knowing your audience and yourself well enough to objectively review your communication skills' effectiveness is critical for a Business Partner.

Growth

Sharing our knowledge through partnering offers the opportunity to grow and deepen our expertise. Translating our raw thoughts in a digestible form means we adapt our expertise to the context. We learn more about the business we support, learn from those we support, and grow by sharing what we know.

We created the ACDC Contextual Partnering Model to describe the four primary functions that Business Partners engage in. The model is useful when helping them to understand which mode to engage in and when.

Figure 2: © The ACDC Contextual Partnering Model

When presented with an issue to work on with a leader or their team, a Business Partner will often need to choose the best type of support required. Those issues can vary from simple to complex and from operational to strategic. This distinction matters because a one-size-fits-all approach does not consider the complexity of the problems or the range of advice required.

There are four modes.

Advising: The Business Partner responds to a particular query or question and advises on the matter. It draws on their expertise and ability to investigate, gather facts, problem-solve and communicate this to the client.

Delivering: This mode is task-focused – a client makes a request, and the Business Partner delivers. Tasks tend to be operational and could include the provision of reports and data or a specific activity.

Collaborating: Here, the Business Partner contributes to an activity or issue together, in partnership with the client, making the relationship more equal. They work together, rather than the Business Partner working independently and then presenting the work to the client. In this mode, the Business Partner is likely to feel integrated with the team.

Coaching: In coaching mode, the Business Partner's role is to prompt and provoke by asking questions that encourage the client to expand their thinking or mindset concerning a particular issue. Coaching is about not providing direct responses but rather assisting the person in exploring ways forward based on their ideas.

Choosing the right mode

So, where do you start in determining the mode of support? The table below provides some guidance, and we look at the modes through the lenses of problem and complexity.

To determine the best support mode, we need to know more about the problem and the possible level of complexity. The most powerful tool you have is a good set of questions. Open-ended questions are the best way to elicit information – even in an undefined problem.

> To determine the best support mode, we need to know more about the problem and the possible level of complexity.

'What' questions:

▶ What has been done to resolve the issue?
▶ What has worked for you?
▶ What has caused this to come about?
▶ What are the risks involved?
▶ What is the best way to communicate this issue?

'Why' questions:

▶ Why has this issue occurred?
▶ Why have other solutions had limited/great success?

▶ Why now?

▶ Why not now?

'Who' questions:

▶ Who are the key players?

▶ What is their impression of the issue?

▶ What are their expectations of you/your team?

▶ How will you demonstrate confidence to them?

'How' questions:

▶ How have you defined the issue?

▶ How do you know you have all the information you need?

▶ How will you communicate this to your team/colleagues/ executive team/Board?

'Where/When' questions:

▶ Where is this issue causing friction or tension?

▶ When will you choose to tackle this issue?

▶ When is the best time to communicate about this issue?

Use these questions to gain deeper insights into your client's issues. They will also elicit valuable information to identify the most effective way to support your client.

1: BACKGROUND & CONTEXT

Here is the Contextual Partnering model overlaid with the problem and complexity axes.

	Low-Medium Complexity level	High Complexity Level
Problem Known	**Delivery** Operational type issues Tend to be quick, repeatable Easy to respond to Simple to understand	**Advising** Technical expertise is necessary Instruction to client Providing experience Your expertise is required
Problem Unknown	**Collaborating** Broader issue (may be undefined) Expertise is not as important Working together to problem-solve The manner/approach required	**Coaching** Vagueness around the problem Questions help to identify the issue Often more than one thing Unique to the client/team

Figure 3: © The ACDC Contextual Partnering Model

The Contextual Partnering model acknowledges the various modes that the Business Partner role can engage in when working with clients and colleagues. It encourages diverse thinking and approaches and reminds us to reflect on where your client is, before engaging with them. While you may have a preferred mode, base your choice on the issue at hand to best support the client.

'Business Partner' implies partnering with the business, but the term differs within and across organisations. For some stakeholders, hand-holding leaders and colleagues and attending to transactional and operational needs are considered a success. In some organisations, the role operates strategically, involved in key decisions and activities alongside the senior team members. The following factors will determine how best the role is utilised:

> 'Business Partner' implies partnering with the business, but the term differs within and across organisations.

1. The willingness of the leader to have a Business Partner as part of their team

2. Leaders with a solid understanding of the value a trusted Business Partner brings to their work and team

3. The preparedness of the client or leader to trust the Business Partner

4. The capability of the Business Partner

5. The system the Business Partner works and how effectively it supports them

6. Transparency and knowledge of business information, strategy and insights.

We will explore these factors in greater detail throughout the book.

A Case Study: Meet Jay

To illustrate the best use of the ACDC Contextual Partnering Model, let us introduce you to Jay. He is a Finance Business Partner at AstraTech, a software engineering company. Jay supports the product development team and its General Manager, Michelle.

Jay has worked with Michelle and her team for two years and has substantially broadened his business knowledge. He now feels he can participate in discussions and on projects even before his finance expertise is required. Jay is often asked for his opinion about specific go-to-market strategies, pricing, sourcing and even new markets. He is an integral part of Michelle's team, and his view is sought-after and valued. Michelle and her team know that they will get a broad and objective view when they seek Jay's advice.

Last Monday afternoon, Michelle asked to see Jay, explaining that she was struggling with an issue and needed his advice. She provided some context – their profitability was slipping and had been so for eighteen months. The CEO and Board were asking a barrage of questions about materials, design and profit margins, and Michelle needed to provide a robust response.

Two years earlier, she forecast that profitability would take a hit because of a contentious acquisition. Michelle felt that the Board and the CEO might be looking for ways to save face, given that most General Managers and

Executives had flagged the decision as high risk at the time.

Jay prepared by jotting down a list of open-ended questions to help him better understand the issue and navigate a way forward for Michelle. He had to be mindful to not go into the conversation with too many questions. Jay recognised that preparation was essential, but overpreparing can stifle the discussion – and, therefore, the solution.

When they met, Michelle gave more context, and, with some good quality open-ended questions from Jay, plus brainstorming and roleplaying, they provided a considered response to the CEO and the Board.

Jay's broad understanding of the business and his knowledge beyond his finance discipline meant that he could collaborate easily with Michelle.

Chapter highlights: the role of the Business Partner

The role of the Business Partner, while more ubiquitous these days, is still often misunderstood. It can come from various business discipline areas, and the Business Partner's experience can range significantly given the lack of formal qualifications or certifications for the role.

Originating in Human Resources (now commonly referred to as the People and Culture function), the Business Partner role evolved almost three decades ago. It developed from a desire to move from operational to more strategic work.

The role continues to evolve in the complex world of business today. The most effective use is when a Business Partner functions as a trusted advisor.

The capabilities of the role centre around:

Expertise (what the Business Partner knows)

Growth (how the Business Partner grows by sharing what they know)

Communication (how the Business Partner can convey what they know).

When providing service to clients, a Business Partner can feel uncertain about where to start. The ACDC Contextual

Partnering Model helps to navigate the discussion with the client and consider what type of mode to engage in when providing business partnering services.

Reflection questions:

How has your role evolved and changed during your time as a Business Partner?

_____

_____

How do you see the role evolving further?

_____

Has your development kept up with the pace of change for the role?

_____

What is your go-to style in the Contextual Partnering Model?

_____

What advice would you have given to Jay in preparing for his meeting with Michelle?

_____

_____

CHAPTER TWO

- - - - - - - - - - - - - - -

Service Model and Systems

A Business Partner will usually be part of a team representing an overarching function such as Finance, IT or HR. This team may include multiple Business Partners and be supported by other roles, such as analysts, advisors and consultants as an example. Business Partners often represent the function that provides services to the business.

The service model influences the way the role is utilised in the business. As discussed earlier, the Business Partner usually has a home team – the department where their business discipline sits, for example, HR or Finance. They will also likely belong to an internal client group, likely a department or a team within a department. Their key clients will usually be the Business Leader and their team, but others may include colleagues from their home team and Business Partners from other business disciplines.

The strength of working relationships with leaders influences the system in which they operate, and many factors can enhance or negatively impact it.

Shared service models

To optimise their effectiveness and productivity, Business Partners also need to be aware of the systems that support them. Essentially this relates to the design of the entire service or ecosystem in which the Business Partner operates.

In larger, more established organisations, the Business Partner provides some service elements but not all. For example, other HR team members will likely cover specialised functions (recruitment and reporting) or less complex inquiries. The Business Partner may be a conduit for these services, introducing their internal clients to colleagues and teams in the department and following up on queries on behalf of an internal client. These Business Partners form part of the service model and can be represented as being connected directly and indirectly. They are likely to relay internal client needs to colleagues in their home team (Human Resources in this example). These colleagues usually sit in what is commonly known as a Centre of Expertise.

> To optimise their effectiveness and productivity, Business Partners also need to be aware of the systems that support them.

A senior leader in a food manufacturing business told us that while the Business Partner was formerly the single point of contact for clients, that function is now performed by the

Centres of Expertise. Unfortunately, this has created confusion in the service model, so the business ensures that the Centres of Expertise communicate with Business Partners to avoid the client needing to repeat their request or brief. This leader also acknowledged that there is never a perfect model for service delivery, but clear communication and keeping client needs at the heart of the model helps to minimise confusion and increases role clarity.

In the following figure, we represent the relationships that exist in the service delivery model.

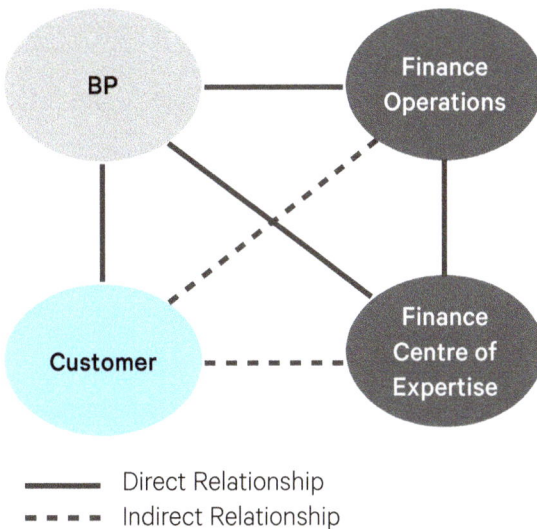

Direct Relationship
- - - - Indirect Relationship

Figure 4: © Relationship between the Service Model and the Customer

The service delivery model may have evolved organically or been designed with a specific purpose for particular requirements. Its effectiveness is demonstrated by the ease with which internal clients can access your services. Is the front door to your service area clear and visible? Do people know who to contact or which system to use to make an enquiry? Are people lost in a maze when enquiring, or is the path for resolution clear and straightforward?

Much can be leveraged and learned through human-centred design when designing, refining, and reviewing service models. Humans are at the core of human-centred design – not technology or existing processes and systems. A service model is designed for human navigation. It is about answering a client query efficiently and effectively with some inbuilt knowledge transfer so that next time they use your services, they are better informed, and their experience is even smoother.

> Much can be leveraged and learned through human-centred design when designing, refining, and reviewing service models.

The value of a well-designed service model

A poorly designed and structured service model makes it difficult for clients to work with Business Partners and their colleagues. A well-designed model considers the organisational needs, business challenges and different aspects of the Business Partner role. It eliminates blockages in the service delivery and enables the Business Partner to add value at a strategic level, more frequently. The following case study explains how this works.

Case Study: Resolving service model issues

A newly formed Finance Business Partnering team had aligned its Business Partners with key clients. They met regularly and responded to client needs. The Business Partner's role was to provide insights and analysis that the client could readily use to inform decision-making. Business Partners had been instructed not to waste their time running reports, or analysing data, as that was the Finance Operations team's responsibility.

The Finance Centre of Expertise comprised specialised finance areas such as tax and reporting with a deep skill set in specific technical areas, whereas the Business Partners were recruited to provide thought leadership. They had direct access and were the conduit between all parts of the service model. One of their primary roles was to ensure communication flowed efficiently between all stakeholder groups.

The Head of Distribution (the internal Client) dealt with serious supply issues, and when suppliers threatened to withhold product because invoices weren't paid within the agreed thirty-day period, the Head of Distribution went straight to the Head of Finance Operations and demanded immediate payment. But the Head of Finance Operations could not authorise payment without first speaking with the Head of the Accounts Payable team (in the Finance Centre of Expertise). They also wanted to run it by the Business Partner, as this was the first time they had heard of this supplier issue. Four days passed before the issue was resolved. By that stage, store shelves were empty and remained so for six days, impacting sales, client satisfaction and store managers who had to deal with frontline customer complaints.

> A well-designed service model considers all potential client needs and includes scenarios for escalation and remediation that clear bottlenecks from the system.

Fixing the service model

In this case study, the service delivery model did not adequately allow quick decision-making or the escalation of issues. The lack of a direct relationship between the internal clients (in this case, the Head of Distribution and the Head of Finance Operations) meant delays, and ultimately no product on the shelves.

A well-designed service model considers all potential client needs and includes scenarios for escalation and remediation that clear bottlenecks from the system. It ensures unhindered accessibility for the client. They should know the services provided and how to access them. As you can see in the following model, the design of the service model should position the service impact at its core.

Service Impact Model

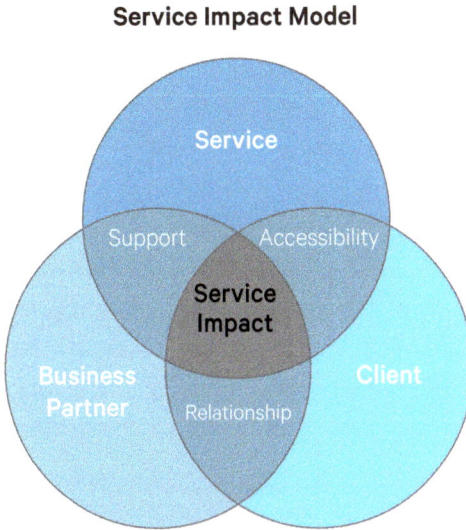

Figure 5: © Service Impact Model

Surrounding it are three key components – the Service, the Client and the Business Partner.

The intersection between the Service and the Client is accessibility. How easily is the service provided understood, accessed and explained?

Between the Client and the Business Partner sits the relationship. The strength of this relationship is often visible in the trust between the Business Partner and the Client.

Support sits between the Business Partner and the Service. It is integral in making the work of the Business Partner easier and providing a better experience for the Client.

Service Impact describes the satisfaction of each stakeholder in the model. Provision should be effective and efficient while maintaining accuracy, quality and a high level of trust and integrity.

Once the Client is defined, the next step is to review current processes. This often presents as a pressing need when something goes wrong. As an internal service provider, you can get ahead by mapping key processes using methods in human design thinking. Where are the blockages and barriers that clients may face? Step outside technology processes here. In the case study above, we can see that the issues were communication, delegations of authority and decision-making. When service issues arise, we tend to look at technology first, but this is not wise.

As we explore service models in-depth, make the user experience the focus of any review or redesign. Don't always start with technology. Is the system adequate if you are offering your clients a solution, such as raising a ticket? Do your internal clients know how to use it? Is it easy to use? Unless the system provides a more efficient, speedier solution, clients may be reluctant to move to a system rather than having a human response to their query.

When designing processes, always test assumptions and potential solutions with your client. Does your solution meet their need? If not, iterate partnering with the client until it does (as far as possible).

The final question is important. Has your service delivery model been communicated to your internal client? It is obvious yet is often forgotten, or worse, ignored. We cannot serve clients if they are unsure what to expect, who to contact or how to resolve their issue. When this occurs, service providers and Business Partners note the lack of trust in the relationship and feel excluded or even irrelevant. Managing change can be relentless and exhausting. In this instance, the role of Business Partners was to navigate and engage with key stakeholders successfully.

From a plethora of change management models, we draw on the research of Sirkin, Keenan and Jackson (Sirkin, Keenan, & Jackson, 2005). Their DICE factors (Duration, Integrity, Commitment and Effort) correlate with the success or failure of change programs.

D signifies the duration of the entire project. It can also signify the duration of smaller projects within a bigger project and the frequency of project reviews.

I is the project team's performance integrity, specifically, their relative capability to complete the project on time.

C represents the commitment to change of senior management and employees impacted by the change initiative.

E shows the discretionary effort required from employees to impact change.

A poorly designed service model makes it difficult for Business Partners to initiate the necessary support for clients and for clients to engage with Business Partners. In contrast, a well-designed model considers the organisational needs, business challenges and the different aspects of the Business Partner role. It eliminates blockages in service and enables the Business Partner to add value at a strategic level.

To test the efficacy of a service model, consider the following questions:

- ▶ What systems are in place to support the work of the Business Partner?
- ▶ What supporting resources does the Business Partner have available to them?
- ▶ How is the role of the Business Partner designed?
- ▶ What expectations exist concerning the service the Business Partner provides?
- ▶ Does the role of the Business Partner operate at a transactional, operational or strategic level?
- ▶ How well-versed are members of, for example, the HR Department on their peers' priorities and focus areas?

Chapter highlights: Service models and systems

A highly competent Business Partner can be impacted when they are operating in a sub-standard service model or system. The support for the Business Partner in a successfully operating service model is critical in ensuring the client receives the best possible service.

The challenge for the Business Partner is that they are often caught in the middle, between their home department, which is part of the service model and their client. The Business Partner plays a crucial role in understanding and translating the parties' needs in the service model. Often, they are best placed to do so because of their deep understanding of their technical area of expertise and their client's needs. They understand the overlap between the client, the Business Partner and the service.

Reflection questions

What service model am I operating in?

_____

_____

_____

Does the service model support my client's needs?

_____

_____

_____

How does the service model support me as the Business Partner?

_____

_____

_____

How accessible are the services for my client?

_____

_____

_____

Does the client know who to contact in accessing services offered as part of the service model?

_____

_____

_____

CHAPTER THREE

- - - - - - - - - - - - - - - -

Navigating Business Partnering Obstacles

Obstacles for the Business Partner

At times, the Business Partner role can be lonely. You may not feel like you belong with your client's team or your home team. Having two masters is another issue that can arise. That dreaded question of 'So, who do you report to?', the dotted and other reporting lines can increase confusion and ambiguity. There is no clear definition of a great impactful Business Partner.

You learn the core capabilities as you develop further and leverage experience from previous roles. There is plenty of learning on the job. While not necessarily bad, it can, at times, make for a confusing development path. You may even question your value and credibility. You may doubt your breadth of business knowledge and what is required to best support the leaders you partner with. Perhaps you are frustrated by the systems and processes that support you. Or maybe you feel disillusioned with the breadth you often need to navigate, from the operational to the strategic. You are also likely to bear the brunt of feedback received about your department, even though you may have little

1: BACKGROUND & CONTEXT

influence over the output of those broader teams. The workload can be intense as you work in multiple groups and often have competing priorities.

Many Business Partners lament that they are not involved in solving strategic issues. They are still waiting to be given a seat at the table. To progress from being irrelevant to highly valued, you can build credibility by consistently demonstrating the value you bring to the organisation, the leader, and the team. This builds trust and assists in demonstrating consistent value.

This chapter will call out several obstacles that can impact the Business Partner's ability to be highly effective and provide guidance on how to deal with them. We'll look specifically at what it takes to work at the strategic level and what you need to maintain your position. We also consider the Business and Business Leader's perspectives and the challenges they may face in accessing the proper support from their Business Partner.

> A Business Partner must continually build, consolidate, and calibrate their commercial acumen to drive business value.

Firstly, let's take a look from the Business Partner's perspective.

Limited understanding of the business

A Business Partner must continually build, consolidate, and

calibrate their commercial acumen to drive business value. Being an expert in one professional discipline is not enough. A great Business Partner moves beyond their technical domain to focus on helping the business to succeed. They are always looking for ways to drive business value.

Business Partners are best served by building relationships at all levels of the organisation and fully knowing each business area. By doing this, perspective on issues becomes clear, and advice is holistic and inclusive. Business Partners also need to look outside of the organisation to build their business knowledge. If we only ever look within our own space, growth opportunities are limited. A Business Partner brings strategic foresight to the role, and looking out into other businesses and industries strengthens commercial acumen and increases your credibility and commitment.

A great way to increase your commercial acumen is to undertake time in another business area – one outside your professional area of expertise. A secondment into another area will enable you to immerse yourself in your client's shoes and those of your colleagues and the external client. It provides a great vantage point to take as you return to your role. Your expertise will be greater and you will provide increased value.

> A great way to increase your commercial acumen is to undertake time in another business area – one outside your professional area of expertise.

How do you build your commercial acumen to navigate broader business conversations with ease and apply it to your area of expertise?

Minding your gap

We have achieved success as Business Partners through our expertise in a business discipline and our understanding of the business. We communicate and advise using this foundation. Our potential is often unknown. We may be unaware of our gaps and blind spots or may want to hide them, as this could be viewed as a weakness and impact our credibility.

> As Business Partners who advise others, not knowing can make you feel exposed and vulnerable.

However, this gap presents a growth opportunity – to consider what is awaiting discovery. Assessing the gap requires vulnerability. As Business Partners who advise others, not knowing can make you feel exposed and vulnerable. Identifying what is unknown creates strength and an opportunity to build knowledge and skill. It turns up the curiosity dial, and you will likely find that you know more than you realised. The willingness to assess this gap is powerful and will deepen your ability as a highly valued and integral Business Partner.

Finding a clear path to commercial acumen relies on understanding your blind spots and not allowing ego to get in the way of constructive feedback on where your advice or client engagement may be lacking.

What you know is foundational to your performance. Without it, there is limited substance, impacting your ability to perform, show up and complete your role.

Your knowledge gaps are your potential. These can deepen your expertise and enable you to perform at the next level. Being open to continual learning keeps you sharp and makes you a better business partner.

There is humility in striving to learn before knowing.

The gap at the intersection of performance and potential is your growth opportunity. Your performance and potential have the opportunity to elevate you as a Business Partner.

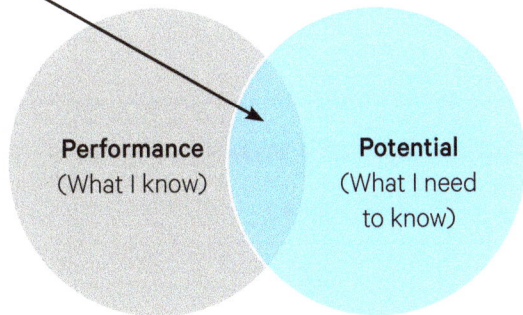

Figure 6: © The gap between performance and potential

> A lack of confidence can negatively impact the Business Partner's ability to build relationships and trust with their Business Leader.

Lack of confidence

A lack of confidence can negatively impact the Business Partner's ability to build relationships and trust with their Business Leader. Often the Business Partner sets the expectation that they should know it all. An HR leader in the health industry reaffirmed that it is important to be 'okay with the ambiguity and not have the answers all the time'. Searching for answers and contributing to solving problems can increase confidence and credibility.

Our research has shown that lack of confidence stems from many reasons, including:

- ▶ Returning to the workforce after a career break
- ▶ Being allocated a new client
- ▶ Changing organisations
- ▶ Increasing business complexity
- ▶ Being in a new team
- ▶ A development gap
- ▶ New technology
- ▶ Negative feedback
- ▶ Changing service models.

Not understanding the value proposition

Struggling to define the value required and the value brought impacts the Business Partner's ability to build relationships. To understand the value proposition, they need to understand the client's requirements and how best to support them. They also need to understand the value they bring to the client. Is it technical expertise? Industry knowledge or experience? Is it their problem-solving ability? Whatever, having a solid understanding of the value proposition helps manage expectations for both parties.

Limited trust

In the next chapter, we offer a value model highlighting the importance of trust and how this grows alongside the relationship between the Business Partner and the client. Yet sometimes trust doesn't develop adequately, and one or both parties may feel the lack. It may have been impacted by an event or never developed sufficiently for a productive working relationship. Limited trust can affect the support provided to the client, leaving the Business Partner disregarded or irrelevant, and the client ignored and unsupported.

> Limited trust can affect the support provided to the client, leaving the Business Partner disregarded or irrelevant, and the client ignored and unsupported.

1: BACKGROUND & CONTEXT

To overcome these challenges and others, consider the following question:

- ▶ What is impacting the relationship between myself and the client?
- ▶ What is my client looking to achieve?
- ▶ Do I have the right level of interest, skills and capability to work with this client?
- ▶ How can I build a relationship with my client?
- ▶ How does my client define value in this relationship?
- ▶ What is the level of trust in this relationship?

Obstacles for the Business and the Business Leader

Having highlighted the issues for the Business Partner, in this section, we consider issues that may arise from the Business Leader's perspective.

Not providing a seat at the table

A seat at the table is a significant symbol for the Business Partner. It is an invitation to contribute equally with other members of the leaders' team. It means their expertise is relied upon and needed as part of creation or problem identification rather than the usual problem resolution.

At times, the Business Partner can be kept at arm's length – called in for specific issues rather than as an integrated team member. This can limit what they are exposed to and their insights about the broader business and the business unit.

When accepted as team members, they access the same information and team dynamics to understand the business differently. Providing this seat at the table helps maximise their effectiveness and impact.

> At times, the Business Partner can be kept at arm's length – called in for specific issues rather than as an integrated team member.

Lack of trust in the Business Partner's expertise

We indicated earlier that limited trust could impact the business partnering relationship. That also applies from the perspective of the Business Leader. A lack of adequate confidence in the Business Partner, particularly in their expertise, will impact the development of the relationship, limiting their understanding of the business and issues at hand. If the leader and their team invest time in becoming familiar with the Business Partner and developing comfort in their level of expertise, this will help them both.

Failure to delegate

Even with sufficient trust and the Business Partner as an integrated member of the team, failure to delegate by the leader will limit and impact the effectiveness of the Business Partner. Lack of delegation happens for many reasons. It may be trust, a perceived capability gap, a belief that doing it themselves will be better or concern for the workload of the person they are considering delegating to. Whatever the reason, the outcome is that the Business Partner is shut out from work that can increase their familiarity and knowledge of the business.

> Even with sufficient trust and the Business Partner as an integrated member of the team, failure to delegate by the leader will limit and impact the effectiveness of the Business Partner.

Unclear scoping requirements

Another issue is that the Business Leader may not always ask for what they need. A senior HR Leader in the sporting industry commented that one of the most significant changes in the business partnering role is that the pace of change and the complex business environment mean leaders can be consumed entirely by what is immediate and in front of them. That can lead to confusion between what is requested and what is needed. Business Partners need to proactively assist leaders to gain greater clarity about their requirements.

To overcome these challenges, we highlight some points of consideration for the leader.

- ▶ Am I clear about what is required from the Business Partner role?
- ▶ How can I best partner with this role and effectively leverage their capability?
- ▶ What tasks and accountabilities can I provide through this role?
- ▶ Do I have sufficient trust and confidence in this person?
- ▶ How can I help this person feel they are a more integrated member of my team?
- ▶ How can I help the Business Partner develop a greater understanding of my business?

Chapter highlights: Obstacles for the Business Partner

This chapter highlighted obstacles that can arise for the Business Partner and the Business Leader. We encourage you to think about how you can effectively take up your Business Partner role in areas such as trust, familiarity with the business you support, and confidence as potential barriers to effective business partnering.

Reflection questions

Are you involved in solving strategic business issues?

_____

If not, what's holding you back?

_____

_____

_____

How can you develop a deeper understanding of your business?

_____

_____

_____

_____

_____

_____

Where is your growth opportunity – between what you know and what you need to know?

_____

_____

_____

_____

_____

Who can you speak to across the business to reduce any blind spots?

_____

_____

_____

_____

_____

Business Partnering Impact Model

Delivering Increased Value

2: BUSINESS PARTNERING IMPACT MODEL

Value in Business Partnering is about understanding the business strategy and how the business creates, delivers and generates value and provides relevant insights into strategy and performance.

Climbing the ladder

The value proposition of the Business Partner can be challenging to articulate because it is all somewhat subjective. What one client deems valuable may be measured differently by another. We developed the following model that demonstrates the growing relationship between the Business Partner and their client.

Trust is the core thread running through the model. As the relationship deepens, so too does trust. With that comes better communication, transparency and service provided by the Business Partner.

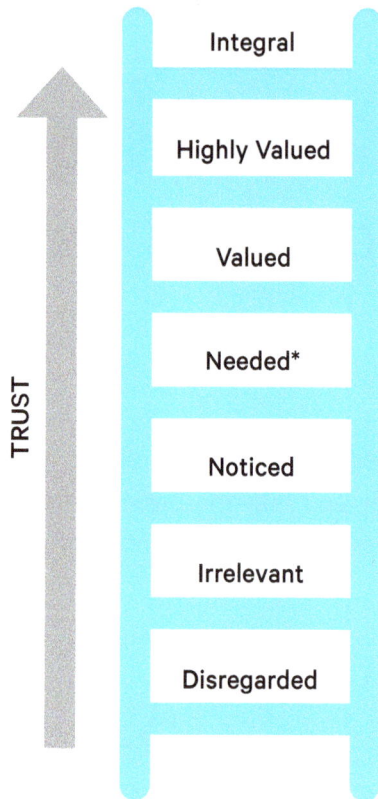

Figure 7: © Relationship between Business Partner and client

Let's consider the capabilities that generate progress up the ladder. Each Business Partner's journey will start at a different point – depending mainly on where their client initially sees them and influenced by where the Business Partner perceives themself. That point is where ego and blind spots can derail the path to the final stage of 'Integral'. You can skip a rung or maybe even two as you proceed, and trust grows with every step. To use the term coined by Maister, Green and Galford, you become the Trusted Advisor (Maister, Green, & Galford, 2001).

When considering the concept of trust, you may think of people you do or don't trust, or of brands and products, and even governing bodies and associations. You may pose the question of who you trust, why and what it represents. In the context of business partnerships, trust is significant. In his book, *The Five Dysfunctions of a Team*, Lencioni says that teamwork begins by building trust (Lencioni, 2002). This applies to any relationship, not just those found in teams. It is about moving into vulnerability, enabling us to be open, genuine and encouraging us to know each other better.

In Figure 7, trust can fluctuate depending on what is said and done. Actions impact trust, such as not honouring commitments, not being responsive and demonstrating a lack of care. Trust can take a while to build and can be lost in an instant.

No Business Partner ever wants to be at the **Disregarded** level. There can be many reasons why your client may not require your support – perhaps they have managed well without the role, or the role is new to the organisation. Whatever the reason, if you are here, don't dwell on it; get off this rung immediately.

At **Irrelevant**, you're not in a much better position, but you are present – and your client knows it. This step is about becoming visible and noticed. Do you know everything needed to support your business and Leader? If not, what are the gaps or blind spots? How do you demonstrate your relevance?

At the next step, you are now **Noticed**. You have developed some credibility and are adding some value. Your client notices your contributions, and you are regarded as the subject matter expert in certain areas. As you demonstrate capability through hard work, these small acknowledgements build confidence in your work. Stay focused; you are one-third of the way up the ladder of trust!

Once you get to the tipping point, you are **Needed**, but it's not time to celebrate just yet! You demonstrate value, as your client needs you across many operational and more strategic activities. You have a strong understanding of your business and the team you support. You have credibility and are viewed as part of the extended team. Your subject matter expertise (depth) is respected, as is your knowledge in other areas (breadth). Needed is good, but not yet great. Let's move to the next level.

You are **Valued**. Your client understands the contribution you make. With your solid commercial acumen, you draw insights using your expertise and knowledge. As your understanding of the business deepens, so your support increases. You receive positive feedback and feel that your contribution is appreciated and respected. The view is excellent from this position on the ladder, but how much better will it look at the remaining steps?

At **Highly Valued,** your input and contributions to the team are well regarded. You know the business inside out. You are constantly learning and evolving your knowledge; you ask insightful questions and are a strong and active listener. You have a high trust relationship with your client and their team, and are seen as a trusted advisor. You exude confidence consistent with a Business Partner who knows their strengths and can say, 'I don't know the answer to that, let me find out for you'.

Integral. You have now reached the top of the ladder and are well and truly part of the team. Everyone has forgotten that you are the Business Partner because you are an essential leadership team member. You have some accountability for business results and work with colleagues on the leadership team to achieve success. You easily navigate discussions, moving between your views on business strategy and your expertise. The uninitiated at the table are somewhat unsure of your core area of expertise – you are too well-rounded to be confined to a particular discipline. Their KPIs are your KPIs. How is the view from the top step?

If you are above **Valued** on the ladder, then well done. If you're not quite here, then consider what you need to do to move up. If you struggle to see what is required, let us introduce you to a model that will help. If you don't know where you are on the ladder, ask your clients and colleagues. Talk about the value you bring to the team. Ask for feedback. It is essential to identify your current spot on the ladder to create a plan to get where you aspire to be.

The table below outlines the value ladder from the perspective of the Business Partner and the client.

Level of trust	What the Business Partner feels	What the client feels
High trust	Integral	Revered
	Highly Valued	Supported
Trust	Valued	Respected
Some trust	Needed	Regarded
	Noticed	Acknowledged
No trust	Irrelevant	Unsupported
	Disregarded	Ignored

Table 1: Levels of trust model

As trust deepens, the Business Partner feels increasingly needed and valued, and the client feels increasing levels of support and understanding. This enhances the working relationship and the outcomes of the service provided.

A Case Study: Expert Soundbites: How is the Business Partner role evolving?

'And at the moment, we're probably professionals deploying a lot of solutions at pace and at scale, being that connector across your own function and across multiple functions has never been so important...the way we do it absolutely matters.' – Kate Klease, Head of People & Culture, Home Trades Hub Australia.

'Be really robust with your time management, to ensure you're able to deliver on your business model. So, what's important is also focusing on your personal development, and especially around that commercial acumen piece. So, constantly being aware of factors that are impacting your clients and the role that you and the team can play in that. So, developing your commercial acumen, and then embedding that through the team is critical to delivering value to your partners.' – Jordan Papadopoulos, Head of Sales & Marketing, Otto – Humanising Technology. (www.ottoit.com.au)

'We looked at analysing and understanding the changes that were happening within our departments, and what our client groups were experiencing. A key thing there is just reviewing the ways we interacted with our stakeholders ensuring that everything we deliver is remaining relevant in the changing environment that we operate in. The key elements of resilience to help our teams navigate through the uncertainty has been a very important part of the business partnering role and that connection back to our mission and purpose.' – Lisa Calderone, Director, People & Culture, Kogan.com.

'The importance of partnering and guidance goes through the entire company, not just at the very senior end. To stand out as a Business Partner, stay relevant. Learn other methods, network, keep an eye on the market and know what's going on and not going to ever be complacent. So you're future-proofing your profile. You really need to know, what good is and what the yardstick is.' – Alex King Co-Founder & Head of Business Partnering, Ledge HR (www.ledgehr.com.au)

2: BUSINESS PARTNERING IMPACT MODEL

Chapter highlights: Delivering increased value

Trust and value are key in the Business Partnering Relationship. In the value ladder, we demonstrated that as trust grows, so too does the perceived value of the Business Partner, as they move from disregarded to integral. During this time, trust and credibility build between the Business Partner and the Business Leader who feels increasingly positive about the relationship. Business Partner increases their sense of worth and value as they move from feeling ignored to potentially revered.

Reflection questions

Where are you on the Business Partner value ladder?

_____

_____

_____

What keeps you at this level?

_____

_____

What level would you like to reach?

What will you put in place to help get you there?

What level of trust exists between you and your client?

What can you do to increase trust?

The Business Partnering Impact Model

In this chapter, we consider a model that can support a Business Partner's development.

As highlighted earlier, there is no formal education path for a Business Partner, which is understandable given there are so many ways to enter the role. To bridge this gap, we have developed the Business Partnering Impact Model. Its application has been integral in our coaching and training sessions and in developing our business model. The model unpacks what the business needs to be best supported by a Business Partner and charts a developmental direction.

> ... there is no formal education path for a Business Partner, which is understandable given there are so many ways to enter the role.

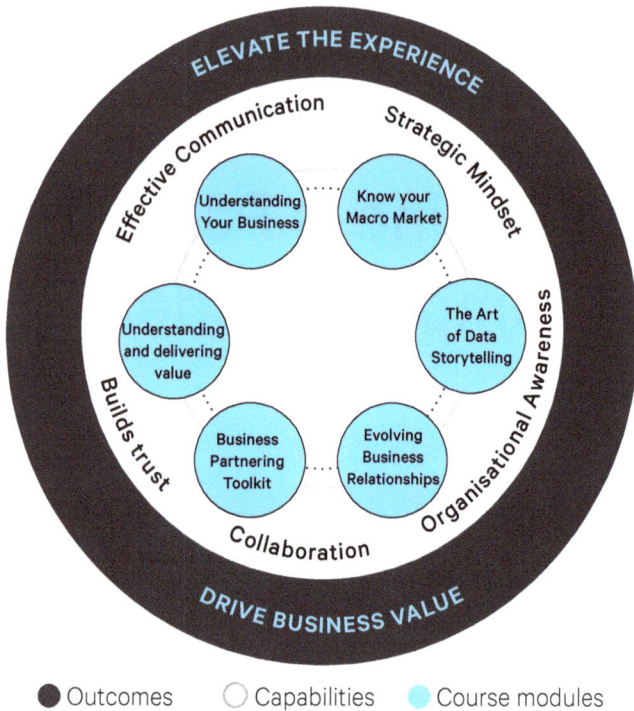

Figure 8: © Business Partnering Impact Program

The outer circle starts with **Elevating the Experience.**

If driving business value describes the 'what', then elevating the experience is about the 'how'. Let's take a client experience (Cx) view of the world. In this case, Cx would be the interaction internal clients have with your team. It is about making those interactions useful and ensuring your processes are easy for clients to follow and use. It is also essential to involve your customers in the design process.

The holy grail of elevating the experience is the powerful belief that continually improving your client's experience will increase advocacy and loyalty.

Next, we focus on **Driving Business Value.**

The Business Partner's number one role is to drive business value. To do so, a Business Partner needs continually to build, consolidate, and calibrate their commercial acumen. Being an expert in a professional discipline is not enough. A great Business Partner moves beyond their technical domain to focus on how to help the business to win – always seeking new ways to drive business value.

Six Essential Capabilities

Our research identified the **Six Essential Capabilities** that make up the next layer. These areas are where Business Partners should invest to grow their influence. To direct their development attention, we've developed the Business Partnering Impact Capability Model. It focuses on six capabilities to drive business value and elevating the partnering experience with the business.

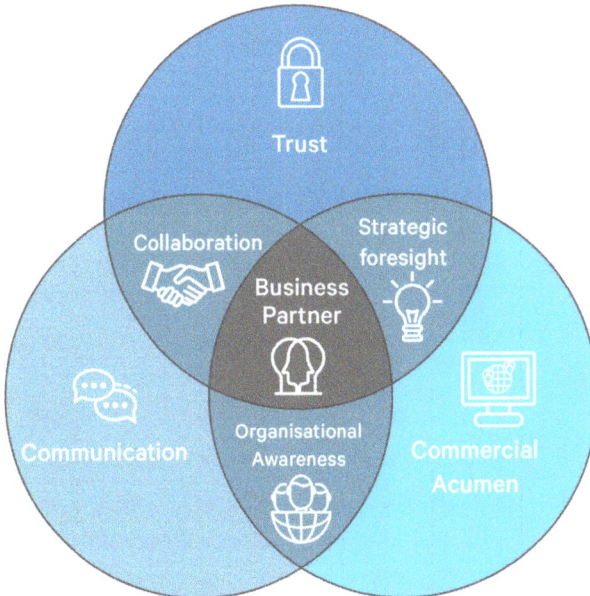

Figure 9: © Business Partnering Impact Capability Model

These capabilities are based on key competency areas and the evolving nature of the Business Partner role.

Capability #1: Communication

It's obvious (but often overlooked) that the ability to listen to our clients and colleagues effectively, consider their needs and requests and formulate strategic advice can be challenging. That is because a Business Partner is there to make the complex simple.

> It's obvious (but often overlooked) that the ability to listen to our clients and colleagues effectively, consider their needs and requests and formulate strategic advice can be challenging.

We wade through problems and complexity, make sense of the issues and impacts, consider all perspectives and then advise. To do so effectively, we need to be fully present and focused on what the person is communicating and what we are learning – rather than thinking about the next action or our follow-up response. This ensures we have given the issue appropriate consideration and thinking required for our advice to be valuable.

We assume that the person has understood our thinking and rationale, yet just because we've communicated something does not mean it was understood. Checking for understanding is vital to ensure that we are engaging in the best method of communication for our audience. Consider also the frequency of communication and the level of detail. George Bernard Shaw said it best, 'The single biggest problem in communication is the illusion that it has taken place.'

Capability #2: Trust

In his book *Principles*, Ray Dalio writes that 'meaningful relationships and meaningful work are mutually reinforcing, especially when supported by radical truth and radical transparency.' Truth and transparency form the basis of trust, which is a priority in any relationship. A lack of trust means no relationship or, at best, an ineffective one (Dalio, 2017).

So, how do you build and maintain trust as a Business Partner? There are several core ingredients: effective communication, delivering on what you promise, demonstrating vulnerability, authenticity and showing empathy. Trust encompasses credibility and reliability and takes time to evolve. It is built and earned by walking your talk.

Earned trust sees Business Partners invited into conversations and given the right to push boundaries, challenge the status quo and

> Trust encompasses credibility and reliability and takes time to evolve. It is built and earned by walking your talk.

encourage lateral thinking. That means they must be willing to take risks.

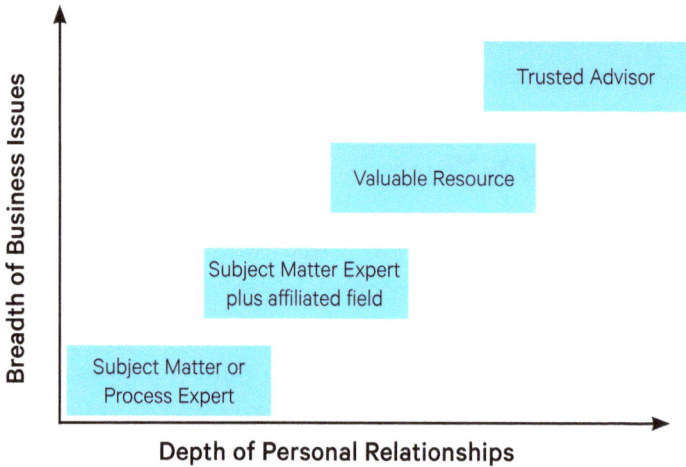

Figure 10: © Becoming a trusted advisor (Maister, Green, & Galford, 2001)

In *The Trusted Advisor*, the authors present a model that shows the relationship between the breadth of business issues and the depth of personal relationships formed as the business partnering relationship evolves. When the Business Partner starts to understand business issues but has limited personal relationships with stakeholders, they may be perceived as a subject matter or process expert. As they develop, they become a valuable resource, then a trusted advisor. Once accepted as a trusted advisor, the Business Partner still needs to work to maintain this status.

Capability #3: Collaboration

The very nature of partnering involves working with others. By sharing ideas, dispelling assumptions, and focusing on goals rather than solutions, you will achieve maximum impact with your clients and colleagues. You can be proactive in presenting independent ideas but ensuring these are open to discussion and debate will raise people's opinions of a Business Partner.

You do not have an automatic right to collaborate on a project with a client. Trust is built over time as credibility and rapport, and provides the context for collaboration. It is an opportunity for co-design, ideation, implementation, and review. The Business Partner progresses from being called in for discrete problems to contributing to larger pieces at the idea stage.

Francesca Gino is a behavioural scientist and Tandon Family Professor of Business Administration at Harvard Business School. She explains six core features that 'crack the code for sustained collaboration'. She says that collaboration can be found and sustained when we:

1. Listen, not talk
2. Practice empathy
3. Find comfort in feedback
4. Lead and follow
5. Speak with clarity and avoid abstractions
6. Focus on win/win interactions.

Whilst not specific to Business Partners, these features are relevant to increasing collaboration in a business partnering relationship (Gino, 2019).

Capability #4: Organisational awareness

Partnering with impact means being attuned to what's happening in and around the organisation. You may be partnering with one area of the business, but broader organisational awareness will enhance your advice. What's happening in other areas of the company? How is the organisation responding to client needs? How profitable is the business? What's the overarching strategy and the individual business unit strategy? These are all questions that Business Partners need to ask and answer to demonstrate their credibility and ability to partner effectively.

One Business Partner shared a simple but embarrassing example of the importance of organisational awareness.

> 'I was invited to attend a meeting, where my leader and I were to update the CEO in her role as executive sponsor of the project we were working on. I arrived early, and the CEO was already in the meeting room. We exchanged greetings, and the CEO asked how I was. I naively answered, 'Really busy!' Rookie error number one. With my false confidence and fast mouth, I shot back with, 'How are you? Good to see the business is doing well!' Her response was, 'We have our challenges as well.' My manager walked in at the end of this very brief exchange, and the meeting commenced promptly.

At the end, my manager and I debriefed, and he asked what the CEO said before the meeting. I shared my exchange and saw the blood rush from his face! 'No, you didn't really say that?' A couple of days earlier, our company had announced the second-biggest loss in its history, and the share price tanked. I'm trying to impress the CEO, and I look like an idiot! As a fast-developing Business Partner, it was a pivotal moment for me and my career. The lesson was clear: make it my business to know the business better than my peers, so I can deliver more business value through my work, and not behave like an amateur!'

Capability #5: Strategic foresight

A strategic mindset requires the Business Partner to plan and move into the future with focused intentions and precise actions. It builds on the organisational awareness capability by looking both inside and outside the organisation. The Business Partner must move seamlessly between operational and strategic perspectives, with a clear and robust view of which initiatives and actions best support the strategy. This will enable them to spot issues

> A strategic mindset requires the Business Partner to plan and move into the future with focused intentions and precise actions.

on the horizon and engage in strategic foresight to bolster their leader and business unit.

These six capabilities form the basis of what makes a trusted partner and advisor in any business.

Capability #6: Commercial Acumen

Developing your breadth of expertise provides immense value for Business Partners, specifically increasing your understanding of the business. We define Commercial Acumen as enhancing decision-making and influencing abilities by developing a solid understanding of the company's business model and the external macro-market influences that impact business viability.

Chapter Five is dedicated to Commercial Acumen, providing further insight into how to develop this increasingly relevant capability.

Practical skills for Business Partners

When designing the Business Partnering Impact Program, we researched the essential practical capabilities required, balancing vital behavioural attributes with refining Commercial Acumen. This section discusses these six holistic skills in detail.

Evolving business relationships

A solid business relationship is based on trust, openness, genuine conversations and feedback. Sustainable, strong business relationships are at the heart of Business Partnering. The partnership you create with your clients and colleagues impacts the way you work and interact. We love the Dutch proverb, 'Trust arrives on foot but leaves on horseback'. Trust underpins any relationship – you know intuitively when you have it and feel it strongly when you don't.

We often think about communication in terms of how is it done, but it's more than that. Having a solid rapport with your client means you'll be able to have the necessary hard discussions. Openness, care and respect in the relationship creates the best environment for genuine conversations.

> Focusing on empathy is a key part of building and maintaining business relationships.

Focusing on empathy is a key part of building and maintaining business relationships. This practice lets you consider how clients are feeling, what they're thinking, what they're hearing and saying, what's causing them headaches and what's giving them joy. When you do this, the relationship improves because you have taken the time to understand before doing anything else.

People do not engender trust when they try too hard, and they're not genuine. It's about playing the long game, achieving small wins and achieving them often. The quality of your work and how you deliver will always prevail, so be intentional in building business relationships. Regard it as a privilege to partner with a leader and their team.

Business Partnering Toolkit

Great Business Partners have a kit of tried and tested tools to help clients generate ideas, further understanding and perhaps see different perspectives. These are leveraged from the disciplines of Project Management, Strategic Planning and Communication, Negotiation, Influencing and Stakeholder Management, and others. Stay current by knowing what is available and be discerning about what you use with different clients. The tools we recommend help you understand your client's needs. Remember that those needs are often not articulated, can be fuzzy and are perhaps a symptom rather than the cause of the background issue. Our programs provide tools to help you get to the core of issues and offer the right advice.

The role of the Business Partner can even vary within a single interaction. At times, you will be asked to deliver, implement, coach, advise, or collaborate. In that interaction, your client may not know what they need from you, so your job includes tapping into your superpowers and working out what best serves the client. To do this means asking yourself, 'How can I best anticipate the needs of my clients?'

The tools you use should fit the client's culture. Will it work in their team? Does it fit with the way they normally work, communicate, and interact? There is humility in striving to learn before you know. That sounds strange when you are the expert providing the advice, but a great advisor will seek to understand fully and use tools thoughtfully to facilitate an outcome.

Delivering and measuring value

One of the most challenging aspects of the Business Partner role can be knowing whether you are adding value and figuring out how to measure it. If you are doing a poor job, you will certainly be aware – negative feedback often finds us faster than positive feedback. But the impact of a good job is harder to measure, mainly because it is subjective, and the effect of your advice may not always be immediately evident.

If you have trusting relationships, then genuine conversations and feedback will form part of your ways of working. These are great ways to measure your value. Another way is through empathy mapping – a concept often used in human-centred design to help us tune into our client's perspective (Tschimmel, 2012). Through this process, we see the world through their eyes, with more ability to consider issues from their perspective.

> If you have trusting relationships, then genuine conversations and feedback will form part of your ways of working.

The best way to create an empathy map is to think of a person you would like to know better. They can be a real person you are dealing with or a fictional character who resembles a stakeholder. Place them in the centre of a page, and from there, ask yourself questions, and jot down the answers in the form of a mind map. What does your persona think, feel, say and do? What are their highlights and lowlights? This will provide a more realistic perspective of their world.

Understanding and discussing your client's expectations helps you understand what represents value for them. Talking with them about their expectations of your role will provide a sense of how they like to work with their team and colleagues (like you) who support the team.

People create stories in the absence of information – it's part of sensemaking – but these can lead to dangerous assumptions, so always test them. As a Business Partner, have open and genuine conversations about expectations. You will know where you stand, and so will your client.

CHAPTER SIX

Building Commercial Acumen

Understand the Business

Let's explore a familiar setting. A leader is engaging in a development discussion with their team member, Sam, the Business Partner. The conversation flows, with nods of comfort from Sam as their development goals take shape, until the Leader adds: 'Sam, for your final development goal, let's focus on building your <cue music> Commercial Acumen.'

Sam pauses, eyebrow raised, 'Ok. So, how do you suggest I do this?'

The Leader replies, 'Well. Get to know the business. Speak to other leaders and understand what they do.'

Ok, so maybe it doesn't play out exactly like this, although we are confident that somewhere along your career path, 'build your Commercial/business Acumen' has made its way into your development plan or that of your team.

While it may be easier to develop the technical elements of your role, the how-to of building Commercial Acumen can be ambiguous. Where do we start? How do we define it in an accessible, systematic and actionable way for Business Partners?

To answer this, we go to Ray Dalio's words: 'The two biggest barriers to good decision-making are your ego and your blind spots. Together they make it difficult for you to objectively see what is true and make the best possible decision' (Dalio, 2017).

> So how do you control the ego and reduce blindspots?

This quote is a wonderful reminder not to let experience get in the way of learning new things about yourself and your organisation. So how do you control the ego and reduce blindspots? The 'I've-been-here-for-years-and-know-the-business-inside-out' fixed mindset is fraught with risk. Organisations constantly revisit their go-to-market strategy as new products and services are introduced and adapted to emerging consumer needs and market sentiment. However, a growth mindset means people believe their talents, abilities, and intelligence are adaptable. They are open to learning new things, better at receiving feedback and taking on new challenges (Gottfredson & Reina, 2020).

Famed English philosopher and sociologist Herbert Spencer wrote that 'the great aim of education is not knowledge but action'. Acquiring knowledge and taking action lie at the heart of developing Commercial Acumen. A growth mindset leads to better alignment of your behaviours around what you need to know (knowledge) and what you need to do (actions) to positively influence a business outcome and leverage this knowledge in all your day-to-day interactions.

In the book *Victory Through Organization*, the term 'Strategic Positioner' highlights the need for HR professionals to move beyond knowing to position the business to win in its marketplace (Ulrich, Ulrich, Kryscynski, & Brockbank, 2017). The research identified four phases to being an effective Strategic Positioner:

1. They master the language and flow of business
2. They recognise and deliver strategy and sources of competitive advantage
3. Understand and co-create with external stakeholders
4. Anticipate and react to external business trends and context.

These four phases are relevant to all Business Partners regardless of discipline. It is no longer enough only to have deep technical expertise in their professional area; they must know about the services and solutions across the entire business and generate insights to inform advice and problem-solving.

In our research, a senior HR leader in higher education described the Business Partner as the bridge between the HR team and the institution. This role facilitates the ease of information between Human Resources (or any other business discipline) and the client group. It also provides a shared cultural understanding of how things get done.

2: BUSINESS PARTNERING IMPACT MODEL

This knowledge enables the Business Partner to gain and maintain credibility with their clients and develop a deeper understanding of the business. But what does 'understanding your business' mean?

Let's start with deconstructing the term 'Commercial Acumen'. The Cambridge Dictionary defines *commercial* as 'relating to business and their activities', 'for making a profit' or the 'focus on an organisation's business activities and ability to generate value and profit'. When considering this, we expand the thinking to include an extensive and complete understanding of how a company creates and delivers value for clients, customers and stakeholders. The Dictionary's broad definition of *acumen* focuses on sound decision-making in a specific area (Cambridge Dictionary, 2021).

To connect and expand the two concepts, we describe Commercial Acumen as 'enhancing one's decision-making and influencing abilities, by developing a strong understanding of your company's business model and the external macro-market influences that impact business viability.'

> Two broad topic areas encompass our definition: First, understand your business model and then understand the world around you.

Two broad topic areas encompass our definition: First, understand your business model and then understand the world around you.

Understand your business model

Our thinking in this area has been influenced by the amazing work of Alexander Osterwalder and Yves Pigneur, who wrote *Business Model Generation*. This practical book helps practitioners understand and enhance their company business model (Osterwalder & Pigneur, 2010).

We've adapted their Business Model Canvas model into a nine-block table with inter-related elements that impact and influence each other and help construct and analyse a company's business model. This simple table will help business partnering practitioners reduce blind spots and increase confidence in their decision-making abilities. The discussion starters in this section are designed as reflections. Complete them alone or in collaboration with your colleagues and Business Partner peers. Note pads and pens at the ready!

Vision and Mission Statement	Value Proposition	Core Business Activities
Target Market	Channels To Market	External Partners
Required Resources / Assets	Expenses	Revenue

Table 2: Adapted Business Model Canvas

Vision and mission statement

Your organisation's vision and mission statement underpins your basic knowledge of the business model and will shape your understanding of how the remaining eight elements are structured to achieve the future aspirations of your organisation (vision), what you exist to do, and whom you serve (mission).

Discussion starters:

Vision:

- ▶ Does your organisation have an existing vision and mission statement and is it still relevant?
- ▶ What are the organisation's future aspirations, hopes and ambitions?
- ▶ What are the organisation's aspirations for community impact and change?

Mission:

- ▶ What does your organisation exist to do?
- ▶ What business are you in?
- ▶ Who are your target markets and segments?

Value proposition

A value proposition is a statement that clearly articulates what your organisation's brand stands for and the promise you make to consumers. It is typically sculpted in conjunction with the marketing strategy and comprises only a few sentences. This business

> A value proposition is a statement that clearly articulates what your organisation's brand stands for and the promise you make to consumers.

model element captures the existing value proposition and helps consolidate your knowledge and structure of the broader business model elements (Cote, 2020). Have an intimate working knowledge of the value proposition and how it might vary by business unit and the products and services offered to the market.

Discussion starters:

▶ Explore the value proposition in more detail – what problem are you solving and for whom?

▶ What unmet customer needs are you addressing?

▶ Is there congruence between the external customer value proposition and your organisation's employee value proposition?

Core business activities

Capture the core business activities of your organisation – what you do to deliver on your value proposition. A deeper understanding reveals the unseen operational elements of an organisation.

For example, analysing the McDonald's Annual Report 2020, you'll observe core business activities to include the obvious; cooking and serving food quickly with consistent customer service and quality. But more broadly, McDonald's also has immense capability in marketing and advertising, digital and technology, logistics, world-class learning and development of staff, property management and franchise management. Together, the scope of their business activities have matured and adapted over time to reflect market needs, generated a sustainable point of differentiation and increased stakeholder value (McDonald's, 2021).

Discussion starters:

▶ What are the critical business activities that help deliver on your value proposition?

▶ How many of these activities are visible to your customer, and how many are unseen?

▶ How have your core activities evolved in recent years with the solid push for the digitisation of business models?

Start a conversation with a marketing Business Partner to share further insight into the target market and its various segments across products or services.

Target market

Consider your target market, the unmet need you address with each segment and how this may vary by product or service. Start a conversation with a marketing Business Partner to share further insight into the target market and its various segments across products or services.

Discussion starters:

▶ What is your target market?

▶ Who are your most profitable customer segments?

▶ How has your customer base changed?

Have specific customer segments become more important over time?

Channels to market

This outlines how an organisation communicates with and reaches its target market to fulfil the value proposition. They serve the purpose of:

- ▶ Increasing awareness of company brand about their products, services and solutions
- ▶ Providing the target market with a means of acquiring your products, services and solutions
- ▶ Allowing the organisation a means of connecting with the target market post-sale for support and feedback.

Examples of channels to market include direct sales teams, website and other digital assets, physical stores, partner stores or wholesalers.

For example, Netflix reaches their current and potential customers via the internet browser on personal computers, smartphones, tablets, smart TVs, mobile app, video game consoles, digital and TV advertising.

Discussion starters:

- ▶ How do your channels to market vary across your various customer segments?
- ▶ Which are your most profitable channels to market?
- ▶ How do you communicate and interact with current and potential customers? How does this vary across segments?

External partners

An essential element of an organisation's business model is utilising external partners and suppliers to enhance their business activity capability and enable the organisation to deliver on its value proposition. External partners comprise strategic partnerships (with direct competitors and non-competitors), joint ventures and traditional supplier arrangements that provide raw materials and supplies.

> External partners comprise strategic partnerships (with direct competitors and non-competitors), joint ventures and traditional supplier arrangements that provide raw materials and supplies.

Discussion starters:

▶ Arrange a conversation with your procurement Business Partner to identify the most important external partners.

▶ Understand how these external partners support your organisation.

▶ Understand how or if the relationship with these external partners has been impacted (e.g. supply chain issues) and how these problems have been overcome.

Required resources and assets

This captures the physical (e.g. buildings, vehicles, technological assets), financial (e.g. cash reserves), IP (e.g. brands, patents, copyrights) and human resources (e.g. employees) required to deliver on the organisation's value proposition.

Discussion starters:

▶ Map your organisation's core resources across physical, financial, IP, and human resources areas.

▶ How do they interact and influence your company's daily business activities and other business model elements?

Expenses

This element focuses on the underlying expenses of the business model and how it varies by department, product or service. Together with the Revenue element, deconstruct your expenses in collaboration with other Business Partners from various disciplines and a finance Business Partner.

Discussion starters:

▶ How predictable are your expenses?

▶ How profitable are your operations?

▶ How have your expenses/cost base changed in the last three years?

▶ Based on future investment, how is your cost structure expected to change in the next twelve months? Three years? Why is this so?

Revenue

Here, we focus on the financial aspects of the business model, outlining various revenue streams by department, product

> A valuable exercise is to engage multiple Business Partners from different disciplines to examine the organisation's financials alongside a finance Business Partner.

or service. A valuable exercise is to engage multiple Business Partners from different disciplines to examine the organisation's financials alongside a finance Business Partner.

Discussion starters:

▶ How predictable is your revenue?

▶ Which revenue streams are the most profitable?

▶ How has the revenue and profitability of the organisation changed in the last three years?

Understand your macro market

This topic can be complicated to navigate, but it doesn't need to be. Business Partners across all disciplines face similar challenges, as they strive to better connect with key stakeholders and help drive business value during disruptive times. While external business demands increase in complexity, we believe there is a strong need to develop an outside-in view of the macro-world around you.

So, what makes the difference?

Dissect and understand the external macro factors that impact your company and the broader industry to generate simple, actionable insights that inform decision-making. This sounds straightforward, but it takes time, effort and commitment. Without a transparent, disciplined process, you will not shift the dial. Here is how you can start.

There are several pragmatic frameworks available to provide the structure to grow your macro-environment knowledge. Many are simple to understand and a good place to start. We see immense value in using the PESTEL Framework, which has seen numerous iterations in the last forty years. The PESTEL Framework categorises the six external environmental factors that are linked and impact the viability and operation of any business (Johnson, Scholes, & Whittington, 2006). Business Partners need to understand the core drivers of change that may influence the broad structure of an industry and the impact these factors have on particular industries, market sectors and organisations.

> There are several pragmatic frameworks available to provide the structure to grow your macro-environment knowledge.

2: BUSINESS PARTNERING IMPACT MODEL

P Political	E Economic	S Social
RULES AND REGULATIONS *Examines political elements that impact your organisation. Includes the laws and regulations you must comply with to operate your organisation*	**TAXES AND BUYING PATTERNS** *Address impacts on current revenue; where the money is coming from. What expenses, laws, taxes and inflation percentages affect the current cash flow.*	**PSYCHOSOCIAL DATA** *A valuable resource is Government census data that provides a macro-analysis of the general population and their societal attitudes and behaviours*
• Data protection law • Regulation and deregulation • Health and safety law • Environmental law • Government Tax policies (tax rates and incentives) • Competition regulation	• Interest rates • Exchange rates • Inflation • Taxes • Demand/supply • Consumer confidence	• Environmental, Social and Governance (ESG) Reporting • Population growth rate • Religion and beliefs • Average disposable income level • Family size and structure • Investing habits • Immigration rates

T Technological	E Environmental	L Legal
DIGITISATION *What technology does your business rely on each day? Factors could include changes in digital or mobile technology, automation, research and development.*	**CORPORATE SOCIAL RESPONSIBILITY** *These factors relate to the influence of the surrounding environment and the impact of environmental aspects.*	**LAWS TO COMPLY WITH** *Understand what is legal and allowed within the countries, states, and territories your organisation operates in. Awareness of changes in legislation and the impact this may have on business operations viability and profitability.*
• Blockchain • Cyber Risk Artificial • Intelligence (AI) and Machine Learning • Internet of Things (IoT) • Virtual Reality and Augmented Reality	• Climate • Environmental, Social and Governance (ESG) Reporting • Carbon footprint	• Employment legislation • Consumer law • Healthy and safety • International as well as trade regulation and restrictions

Table 3: Adapted PESTEL Framework

2: BUSINESS PARTNERING IMPACT MODEL

Discussion starters

▶ Workshop the PESTEL Framework with colleagues.

Identify your macro-environment knowledge gaps by speaking to leaders and your Business Partner peers across the business to understand more about their knowledge-gathering habits and where you may be lacking. What do they read? Who do they speak to? What do they listen to?

> Whether pitching an idea, communicating a new strategy, or engaging with colleagues, effective storytelling serves an important role in the workplace and any change process.

Build your data and analytics storytelling muscle

Whether pitching an idea, communicating a new strategy, or engaging with colleagues, effective storytelling serves an important role in the workplace and any change process. Stories focus people and make it easier to understand information, particularly with competing interests and focus areas. Research supports the idea that stories can reduce defensiveness, teach complicated concepts, change individuals' behaviour and promote social change (Falk, 2021).

As a Business Partner, regardless of discipline, there is immense value in building confidence using financial and non-financial data to increase impact and engage with stakeholders. In their book *Made to Stick: Why some ideas survive and others die*, authors Chip and Dan Heath summarised it best, 'To make our communications more effective, we need to shift our thinking from "What information do I need to convey?" to "What questions do I want my audience to ask?"' (Heath & Heath, 2008).

It's hard to find more time when presenting analysis to key stakeholders, so focus your attention and resources on solving two key questions. What is the most reasonable course of action based on available information? And what variables can I influence to achieve a business objective? This approach becomes a symbolic North Star, guiding you towards a desired business destination or outcome in a more effective and efficient manner, and enabling leaders to make decisions.

So, where do you start your data and analytics storytelling journey? What questions can you ask to better understand a situation?

Firstly, every story has a hero. Depending on your audience, there will be typically three types of heroes – your external client, employees, and key internal clients. Pick one. Source the data. Share their story. Remember, employees and clients are at the heart of everything we do.

Secondly, whether you are a Finance, Procurement, IT, Marketing or HR Business Partner, you must develop a more holistic view of the quantitative and qualitative data readily available to you, as this directly impacts your internal clients.

2: BUSINESS PARTNERING IMPACT MODEL

The easiest way to do this is to engage with Business Partners from other disciplines tasked with supporting the same business as you. Compare Key Performance Indicators (KPIs), risks and opportunities. What data do they reference in their day-to-day work that informs their decision-making and that of their stakeholders? You may be surprised to find commonality in key performance indicators with these colleagues. This will strengthen working relationships and help point everyone in the same direction.

> Ask better questions to understand your company's or internal stakeholder's financial story.

Ask better questions to understand your company's or internal stakeholder's financial story. Our work with Business Partners involves taking a fresh and practical perspective on data and analytics. No statistics degree is required. Using a simple framework, we explore various phases of data and analytics – from helping construct a narrative of the past (What happened?) and envisioning a possible future (What's likely to happen if we do X?).

Figure 11 aims to prepare you to answer these questions: What do you make of this as a Business Partner? What are your observations? Are there any blind spots? What are the priority considerations?' This is the moment when you have your ticket and are ready to play.

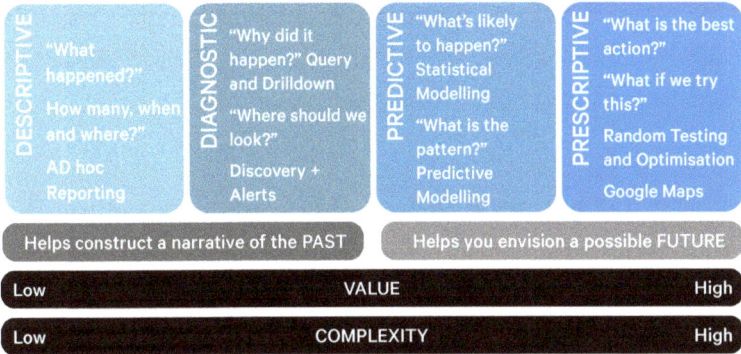

DESCRIPTIVE	DIAGNOSTIC	PREDICTIVE	PRESCRIPTIVE
"What happened?" How many, when and where?" AD hoc Reporting	"Why did it happen?" Query and Drilldown "Where should we look?" Discovery + Alerts	"What's likely to happen?" Statistical Modelling "What is the pattern?" Predictive Modelling	"What is the best action?" "What if we try this?" Random Testing and Optimisation Google Maps

Helps construct a narrative of the PAST	Helps you envision a possible FUTURE

Low	VALUE	High
Low	COMPLEXITY	High

Figure11: © Four types of data and analytics

This widely used model provides a beginner's guide to understanding data and analytics. It is very practical and a useful place to start.

Let's further explore the Four Types of Data and Analytics

What happened? Descriptive analytics

Descriptive analytics in reports capture what happened. Typical metrics included in these canned (or fixed) reports and dashboards are the high-level performance indicators of any business.

An example of a canned report includes information provided to HR Business Partners on attrition rates, open recruitment positions, and the percentage of development plans completed across their business. They also enable further drilling down – for example, the attrition rates in a particular geography or business unit. When coupled with data mining or data aggregation, descriptive analytics starts building a meaningful analytics strategy, describing what has happened in the past. Whilst low complexity and (in isolation) low value, it is the start of bigger things.

Why did it happen? Diagnostic analytics

Diagnostic analytics, like descriptive analytics, help construct a narrative of the past. The added insight is the ability to understand why something happens, trigger a cause-and-effect investigation, identify outliers, pinpoint patterns, or understand relationships between two variables using simple regression analysis.

For example, let's assume your company releases a swimwear line, and you ask your sales manager to forecast sales revenue in the first month of summer. They will respond that it depends on the positioning of stock in the retail stores, market awareness of our e-capabilities, the effectiveness of the marketing campaign, the quality of our competitors' stock, brand awareness and whether it rains in the first month of summer!

> Diagnostic analytics, like descriptive analytics, help construct a narrative of the past.

Regression analysis is a way of ascertaining (in this case, given the high number of factors that can influence sales revenue for the new range) which variables have the greatest impact on a particular outcome. Some models, such as linear regression, are simple to use and understand. Other more complex analysis, such as logistic regression or decision trees, helps address less straightforward questions.

What's likely to happen if? Predictive analytics

Predictive analytics is the start of helping you shape descriptive and diagnostic analytics into actionable insights for forecasting and decision-making. Using predictive modelling, a data analyst could use predictive analytics to shape a view of what is most likely to happen if certain conditions are achieved. For example, 'Based on Q2 results in 2019, when we released our summer footwear range, our online sales increased by 20 per cent.' This approach helps determine trends and patterns and informs business decision-making – impact on staffing, operations, technology, marketing, sales, and finance.

What is the best action if? Prescriptive analytics

Prescriptive analytics is where the expertise of data analysts can help build on predictive analytics and make recommendations on the best (prescribed) course of action. Data analysts are increasingly essential in organisations, building the knowledge bridge between the past and future. Understanding predictive analytics at its basic level means using data from the past to inform actions and decisions for

> Data analysts are increasingly essential in organisations, building the knowledge bridge between the past and future.

the future, helping answer the important question of how we best direct our resources and effort.

Your role is to translate insights into stories that stakeholders can understand. The more depth of knowledge in your Commercial Acumen toolkit, that is, how well you know your business and the world around you, the more effective you will be at connecting and communicating with stakeholders, to let them know why something occurred and the best course of action to take.

So, how can Business Partners start their data analytics journey? Let's deep dive into this next case study.

Case study: Let's talk about data and analytics

To better understand and demystify the world of data and analytics through an expert's eye, we spoke with Gerhard Diedericks, a leading people analytics expert and the founder of Matesis (www.matesis.com). We asked about the importance of predictive models, how data and analytics can create a competitive advantage for businesses and for any tips and recommendations for Business Partners starting their data and analytics journey. This is what he told us.

'Predictive models are about teaching machines to predict, and in some cases, to make decisions. Countless decisions are made in organisations every day: who to recruit, who to promote, how much to pay, which product to offer, and which loan to approve. Teaching machines to make these decisions, or augmenting the decision-making process of human managers, offers significant benefits. Decision machines can do it faster: a loan can be approved instantly, or a job offer made in a few hours. Being faster than your competitors is a competitive advantage, especially when competing for the same resources. Decision machines can also do it more accurately; well-built machines can process more inputs and ignore bias and noise better than human decision-makers.

'Even minor improvements in speed and accuracy can make a difference to a customer's experience with your brand. There is a dark side though, poorly-built machines

2: BUSINESS PARTNERING IMPACT MODEL

can cause much damage – both financial and reputational. Those inaccuracies perpetuate if your decision machine is trained using the wrong methods or on biased and noisy data. Business Partners need to understand how decision machines (predictive models) are built, trained and maintained.'

How do businesses create a competitive advantage with data and analytics?

'Smarter decisions made faster create better experiences for customers and employees. Customers are matched with better products, get better recommendations, and transact easier, increasing loyalty. Employees benefit from faster, fairer and better quality decisions shaping their experiences, and create higher levels of engagement. Loyal customers and highly engaged employees translate into superior returns for investors.'

Mindsets – where do Business Partners start their data analytics journey?

'Business partners are vital links between the deep expertise of data scientists and business requirements, translating business-speak into analytics-speak and vice versa. Deep technical expertise is not essential, but adopting the following five mindsets at different times will prove helpful. Think through the lens of one of these professionals:

A business owner: How do you convert human behaviour into value for customers, employees, shareholders and the community? Be a keen student of customer and employee behaviour.

A scientist: How do you understand how to gather, process and assess the evidence? Be sceptical, curious, do not take anything for granted, and question everything.

An engineer: How do you hack and iterate your way through prototype after prototype, continually improving your model's decision-making capabilities? There is no perfect answer, only models that work a bit better than previous ones.

A teacher: How do you upgrade or augment the mindware of human decision-makers with great storytelling and visuals that reveal the inner working of your decision machines? Insight and understanding should never be outsourced to machines.

A philosopher: How do you think through the ethics of your analytics project? Not every question that can be answered should be answered, especially when sensitive data and privacy issues come into play.'

2: BUSINESS PARTNERING IMPACT MODEL

Reflection questions

The organisational capability of data and analytics should not operate in a silo, but should be embedded into operational structure and processes. The following questions aim to better guide Business Partners to navigate the world of data and analytics through the power of collaboration and curiosity:

How mature is your organisation's data and analytics capability?

_____

_____

What area(s) of the business does data and analytic capability sit?

_____

_____

How are decisions made?

_____

_____

How will you invest in your data and analytics development?

_____

How can you collaborate better with colleagues who have strong data and analytics expertise?

Can you identify an important business problem that you understand in detail and needs to be solved?

Can you use analyse any new data sources to help you understand why it is happening and identify clear next steps?

PART THREE

Navigating the Future

CHAPTER SEVEN

The Impact of Change on the Business Partner Role

At the start of the book, we highlighted that the Volatility, Uncertainty, Complexity and Ambiguity (VUCA) world of business creates opportunities and challenges for the Business Partner.

Over the past eighteen months, we have seen a significant change due to coping with the global pandemic. Throughout this time, Business Partners needed to quickly respond to a new set of changing circumstances and adapt and change at an individual level while often leading and supporting the leadership of this crisis.

Throughout 2020, we conducted weekly workshops to support leaders and interviewed business leaders from various industries and countries to understand the impact of COVID-19 on the Business Partner role.

We asked leaders the following questions:

What was the greatest change in the role of the Business Partner during 2020?

How will the Business Partner role change in the future?

What new skills or competencies do you and your team need to develop?

What business partnering capabilities do you see increasing in importance as a result of the global pandemic?

Here is a summary of what those leaders shared with us.

> Most said that one of the biggest changes to the Business Partner role during 2020 was developing Commercial Acumen.

Commercial Acumen

Most said that one of the biggest changes to the Business Partner role during 2020 was developing Commercial Acumen. Business Partners were required to understand the whole business as never before. The pace at which decisions needed to be made, reviewed and modified meant that a solid grasp of the business was essential, and this was not limited to the domain that the Business Partner offered. HR needed to understand Finance in more detail,

IT needed to understand the company's Sales and Marketing activities, and Finance needed to understand the HR activities designed to support colleagues. It brought about a deeper understanding of the business across all areas.

We saw a shift in strategy, with long-term planning shortening significantly and responding to changing needs and work practices. During the onset of COVID-19, many leaders shared that they felt powerless for the first time in their careers and were not productive, despite their years of experience. In response, businesses put in place cross-functional teams to adequately respond to issues arising from the pandemic. With shorter time horizons, these cross-functional teams had to understand at a deeper level the complexity of how the business runs, not just their part in it. This required whole-of-business responses to ensure that all perspectives were considered and addressed. One positive consequence of this 'coming together of minds' is that relationships have deepened between teams, with opportunities for cross-functional collaboration to be sustainable.

Adaptability and agility

Adaptability was often mentioned in terms of the new skills or competencies that Business Partners required to develop in 2020 and 2021. Adaptability is hard to learn and apply unless the right circumstances arise, so perhaps there has never been a more significant time to learn it on the job and in life in general. The ability to lead through change, and be transparent with others while doing so, can be challenging. **Pivot** will be remembered as the most overused word of 2020, yet it is exactly what occurred. Out of necessity, we all changed what we did and how we did it – usually with no control over the timeframe needed for changes. There was almost a forced agility. For many people and organisations, new ways of working have enhanced their lifestyle.

The two ongoing challenges will be:

1. Sustain these positive enhancements and ensure a business and personal benefit.
2. Let go of behaviours and habits that have served Business Partners well in the past but will not necessarily meet their needs (or business needs) moving forward.

Resilience and mental health issues

Adaptability was almost always accompanied by its friend – resilience. Most people had to further develop it in 2020 (and we continue to). For Business Partners, resilience was critical because of the many knocks and setbacks for businesses and individuals. They needed to help the business, leaders and colleagues to navigate the unknown at every level. Leaders and Business Partners describe playing key roles in supporting those with mental health challenges, placing an enormous burden on themselves as they too navigated hurdles. At first, adequate support to assist was not available, as the external environment moved so quickly. Leaders and Business Partners had to use their personal experiences and available resources such as Employee Assistance Programs to help employees and colleagues to survive, let alone thrive. Business Partners had to coach business leaders and saw the need continue far into the future. This included enabling and facilitating leaders to do their work and find solutions to novel problems rather than take things on directly as Business Partners. This issue is not unique to the pandemic but is ongoing for Business Partners.

Many cited the need to find innovative and creative ways to keep people connected through the challenges of suddenly working from home and adapting to a different work style. Business Partners further supported this by adopting the role of culture and engagement ambassadors or champions. This is about having a sense of the 'How' and the 'What'.

'How' considers the dynamics of the team and the organisation. How are things being done? How is communication occurring? How are the team and colleagues responding? '

'What' is about the actual work – at an operational and mechanical level. What are the business objectives? What is the business strategy? What are the projects or day-to-day work requirements? The role of the Business Partner in the pre and post-pandemic world is to ensure equal focus on both to maximise success.

Colleagues suddenly became more vulnerable with each other as lines that often demarcate work and personal life dissipated. We were in each other's kitchens, living rooms, studies, bedrooms, balconies and gardens. We met family members with impromptu appearances and sounds. Perhaps an unintended positive consequence is that it helped forge stronger working relationships between colleagues by unintentionally dialling up vulnerability. For Business Partners, this was seen as a benefit in building and strengthening relationships with colleagues, and it helped with stakeholder management and developing a deeper trust with colleagues.

Research from TNS Global and Beyond Blue (TNS, 2014) has found that mentally healthy workplaces are as important to Australian employees as physically safe workplaces. Their unique findings include that 91 per cent of employees believe mental health in the workplace is important, whilst 88 per cent believe physical safety is essential.

Despite this, only 52 per cent of employees believe their workplace is mentally healthy compared with 76 per cent for physical safety. Unfortunately, only 56 per cent believe their most senior leader values mental health.

> In HR, our findings demonstrated a clear shift from the traditional approach of directing employees to employee assistance programs.

How does a Business Partner navigate the complex path of mental health in the workplace? One senior HR leader from a major Australian retailer told us that profound mental health challenges in the community require more than technical expertise. He commented that human connection is critical in dealing with these issues and described it as a significant change in the business partnering role.

In HR, our findings demonstrated a clear shift from the traditional approach of directing employees to tailored or enhanced employee assistance programs. Employers are establishing more robust formal and informal data gathering systems related to employee mental wellbeing. These enable Business Partners to connect proactively with their peers for a more preventative approach.

Data, insights and storytelling

We rely on various media to obtain insights that inform our decision-making. Knowing what is credible and can be trusted becomes increasingly difficult with so many choices available. Leaders and Business Partners shared that having relevant and accessible data and insights was critical in assisting decision-making and ensuring that reactive responses were still strategic and well-considered. This will grow in importance as we learn how to test credibility and use stories to enhance communication. Business Partners must consider multiple perspectives, business impacts and have the foresight to think forward, plan adequately and execute effectively.

Business Partners and Leaders were often required to be vulnerable and share what they knew, sometimes with no clear answer or well-considered plan about responding. Given the unpredictable environment, transparency in communication was expected and appreciated throughout 2020, helping to build trust and strengthen relationships.

Change architects

Leaders and Business Partners believe their role as change architects became increasingly significant during 2020 and will continue so as Leaders grapple with adapting and responding to further changes that make us sustainable in a COVID-

3: NAVIGATING THE FUTURE

normal world. It has not been easy to develop skills to navigate and communicate changing legislation and public health guidelines while retaining employment engagement. Solid trust, transparency, and clarity in communication have been necessary to support the increasing importance of leading in a rapidly changing world.

Chapter highlights: How does a Business Partner increase their impact in a COVID-normal world?

Leaders and Business Partners have similar focus areas that require upskilling and attention in 2021. We support these sentiments and encourage all Business Partners to review their performance and impact against these areas. But be realistic, pragmatic and kind to yourself! Many capabilities will be obvious as they cover the underpinning competencies of a Business Partner role.

Reflection questions

The following questions may help increase your impact as a Business Partner in a COVID-normal world.

How well do I know my organisation? Do I know about how the business operates and how it survives?

_____

_____

How am I supporting my internal clients? Am I demonstrating empathy? Do I have a view of their world from their perspective?

_____

3: NAVIGATING THE FUTURE

_____

_____

Am I using data and insights adequately to support my ability to communicate?

_____

How am I supporting wellbeing and mental health issues for my colleagues?

_____

_____

_____

Am I equipped to provide initial support, and do I know where to refer if necessary?

_____

_____

Do I have a self-care plan to maintain my physical, social and mental wellbeing?

_____

_____

_____

Afterword

Throughout this book, we have outlined how the role of the Business Partner has continued to evolve and change.

The evolution of business partnering has been prominent in the increased business disruption and market uncertainties faced globally. Business Partners face heightened expectations, and we are all experiencing significant challenges as we work through unprecedented issues and circumstances.

It's hard to give a clear definition of what makes a great Business Partner, but you know when you have a great one – and when you don't. A valuable Business Partner contributes to a broad range of initiatives outside their area of technical expertise because they have a strategic mindset and deep organisational awareness. They draw insights from complexity and communicate ideas eloquently and simply. They are personable, with a genuine interest in collaboration, and know that trust underpins all relationships. Above all, they work intently to drive business value and ultimately make the business better.

In this book, we have taken you through the evolution of business partnering. It's a role that changed over the past three decades and will continue to do so. While the strategic requirement of the role is not new, it now comes with a renewed vigour. Given our complex world, the Business Partner must have an in-depth knowledge of the business they support and the industry in which they operate.

We discussed how complexities in the service model and systems in which the Business Partner operates, make partnering more challenging. Taking time to simplify these makes it easier for the Business Partner and the clients they support.

> The unexpected pandemic has severely disrupted the business world and brought increased accountabilities for Business Partners in adapting quickly to changing circumstances.

We introduced you to a value model – represented as a ladder that supports the evolution of the Business Partner. Intentionally moving upwards takes you from disregarded to integral and provides the credibility necessary to participate in critical discussions and influence business decisions. We also shared our business partnering capability framework, which represents the balance of relevant behavioural attributes and Commercial Acumen. Both improve the business partnering experience and drive superior business value.

We acknowledge that there can be issues for the Business Partner and the Business Leader as they develop their relationship and build trust and value.

Understanding these issues can remove any tension from the relationship, particularly in the earlier stages.

The last two years have potentially been the most difficult that current generations have had to face. The unexpected pandemic has severely disrupted the business world and brought increased accountabilities for Business Partners in adapting quickly to changing circumstances. Business Partners have needed to operate in ambiguity, high stress and significant change.

The pressure of the pandemic has created the need for Business Partners to lead and manage change while adapting and developing resilience at an individual and organisational level. This has not been easy but has increased the credibility of the role across all stakeholder groups.

We have provided case studies and reflection questions throughout the book.

As Ray Dalio writes in his book, *Principles*, 'The two biggest barriers to good decision-making are your ego and your blind spots... together, they make it difficult for you to objectively see what is true and to make the best possible decision' (Dalio, 2017).

We encourage you to build the capabilities necessary to move up the value ladder to being an integral Business Partner. That is when you will know that the business values and needs what you bring. This is the essence of the evolution of business partnering – it is about Commercial Acumen applied strategically to improve business results.

It is imperative to know the business you support very well. In-depth knowledge and understanding sets you apart, adding value beyond your area of expertise and helping solve broader business issues. Start blurring the lines across business partnering disciplines. Good stuff will happen when you invest in building a community of like-minded problem-solvers, getting into the same (virtually or in-person!) room, and starting sharing information, stories, challenges and opportunities. Compare KPIs – you might be surprised to see the commonality of goals, particularly if you have similar stakeholders across the business. Cross discipline collaboration works, it is working out what your role is in this process – are you the active connector or passive observer?

The key to building great business relationships is not dissimilar to establishing any connection. Plenty of self-awareness coupled with compassion, kindness, patience, and understanding will have you on your way to building relationships that last. Try to be interested and not interesting, and be humble enough to learn when things go wrong. Know that, as with most good things in life, achieving quality takes time.

Call To Action

We hope that this book ignites a spark to act, to grow and to develop. Remember, your brand as a Business Partner is your currency – do invest in it wisely. The wonderfully powerful adage, 'Your personal brand enters the room before you do,' captures the essence of nurturing and growing sustainable partnerships with your colleagues and Business Partner peers.

Start connecting pro-actively with your Business Partner peers. Tap into the immense power of collaboration to realise the aspirations for your organisation in a sustainable and action-oriented manner and realise your potential for growth. There is tremendous power in the diversity of thought and networks. Your investment in self-development starts with awareness of where you focus your energy and time. We suggest starting with these four exploratory questions:

> **Your investment in self-development starts with awareness of where you focus your energy and time.**

1. What do you want to be known for?
2. What makes you unique as a Business Partner?
3. How will you stand out?
4. What kind of leader do you want to be?

Taking ownership of your self-development requires focus and a targeted learning plan. Where do you start? Which websites, blogs, podcasts, virtual mentors, books and social media do you consume? The learning sources are endless and inevitably confusing, so identify a mix of content sources that aligns with your professional and personal lifestyle. 'I-don't-have-enough-time' has stunted many growth plans. Think laterally and creatively. If you walk the dog for twenty minutes, five times per week, source and schedule an audible book or podcast. That's

100 minutes per week of nourishing content, or 5,200 minutes per year or roughly 86 hours of targeted learning.

In his book *Tools of Titans*, Tim Ferris shares the routines and rituals of world-class performers and found that targeted focused learning is a common behavioural trait for many. The book demonstrates it involves more than locking in time; a slow, deliberate approach generates the discipline to change behaviours and develop new habits. Consistency is the key (Ferris, 2017).

So where do you start?

Start with action. Nothing is achieved without it.

> Start with purposeful learning and personal growth – it can be a powerful force for good and can be daunting.

Start with purposeful learning and personal growth – it can be a powerful force for good and can be daunting. Start with curiosity, intrigue and self-awareness. Don't be limited by your fears and doubts.

Start with the process of self-discovery. Start with a bunch of firsts – a first question, a first time, and a first step. Start with Now. However, be considered and deliberate in your actions. Remember the Chinese proverb, 'Be not afraid of going slowly, be afraid only of standing still.'

The expectations of Business Partners are evolving and with these come the need to refresh and upskill. We are passionate about helping people be more confident and excel at what they do.

If you would like to further your development as a Business Partner, visit www.impactology.com.au where we share programs, solutions, podcast and resources. Or email us at: hello@impactology.com.au

We love connecting people in ways that spark new ideas and help them achieve their goals faster. We love a good Business Partner story and would love to hear yours and how you're creating impact.

We wish you well on your business partnering journey.

About the Authors

Rita Cincotta

Rita is an author, speaker, coach and facilitator focused on team and individual performance, leadership development and ways of working. She works with organisations to help them develop a culture that delivers an optimal experience for their teams and customers.

Rita has led teams and held C-suite equivalent roles in Human Resources in various industries, including technology, health, financial services and higher education. As a highly experienced Executive Coach, she has worked with leaders at all levels across most sectors. Rita also serves on the Board of Peninsula Health in Victoria, Australia.

Her goal is to help people to live better, work smarter and be authentic. Rita's clients describe her as innovative and pragmatic, while her family say she is nurturing and impatient. Rita says she is an eternal optimist – curious about different perspectives.

Rita believes that the Business Partner role is a privileged position that immerses itself in the business and creates initiatives that support the overarching strategy. In doing so, they gain new perspectives that strengthen advice and support provided to leaders.

Connect with Rita on LinkedIn or email her: rita@ritacincotta.com

George Liberopoulos

George is an author, speaker, podcaster and pragmatic consultant with more than twenty-five years commercial, HR, and Reward experience.

George has a unique blend of expertise, helping companies and people grow in a disciplined and sustainable way and deliver on their aspirations. George has held C-suite positions, as Chief Commercial Officer at Aon. As a highly experienced Reward consultant, George delivered professional rewards advice to clients across many broad industry sectors, including technology, banking, financial services, food & beverage, engineering and not-for-profit.

George is inspired by storytelling that allows people to grow, learn and be better. Formula 1 is his passion, cinema is his release, futsal and cycling keep him fit, trusted friends are a treasure, and family is everything.

This book is his call to all Business Partners, to evolve, develop and unite. Break down the real or perceived barriers to building strong business relationships and collaborate to drive greater impact.

Connect with George on LinkedIn or email him: george@impactology.com.au

For more information about our programs, podcast, consulting services and our Business Partnering Impact Program, please connect with us.

www.impactology.com.au

https://www.facebook.com/ImpactologyAust

https://www.linkedin.com/company/impactology

References

Bennis, W. G. (1986). *Leaders: The strategies for taking charge*. New York: Harper & Row.

Cambridge Dictionary. (2021, July). Retrieved from Cambridge Dictionary: https://dictionary.cambridge.org

Cote, C. (2020, July 28). *How to Create an Effective Value Proposition*. Retrieved from Harvard Business School Online: https://online.hbs.edu/blog/post/creating-a-value-proposition

Dalio, R. (2017). *Principles: life and work*. New York, N.Y.: Simon & Schuster.

Falk, E. (2021, June 27). *Op-Ed: Why storytelling is an important tool for social change*. Retrieved from Los Angeles Times: https://www.latimes.com/opinion/story/2021-06-27/stories-brain-science-memory-social-change

Ferris, T. (2017). *Tools of Titans*. Boston: Houghton Mifflin Harcourt.

Gino, F. (2019, November-December). *Cracking the Code of Sustained Collaboration*. Retrieved from Harvard Business Review: https://hbr.org/2019/11/cracking-the-code-of-sustained-collaboration

Gottfredson, R., & Reina, C. (2020, January 17). *To Be a Great Leader, You Need the Right Mindset*. Retrieved from

Harvard Business Review: https://hbr.org/2020/01/to-be-a-great-leader-you-need-the-right-mindset

Heath, C., & Heath, D. (2008). *Made to Stick: Why some ideas survive and others die.* New York: Random House.

Johnson, G., Scholes, K., & Whittington, R. (2006). *Exploring Corporate Strategy: Text & Cases 7th Edition.* Hoboken, NJ: Prentice Hall.

Kofman, F. (2006). *Conscious Business: How to Build Value Through Values.* Boulder, CO: Sounds True.

Lencioni, P. (2002). *The Five Dysfunctions of a Team: A Leadership Fable.* San Francisco: Jossey-Bass.

Maister, D. H., Green, C. H., & Galford, R. M. (2001). *The Trusted Advisor.* New York, NY: Simon & Schuster.

McDonald's. (2021, July). *Annual Report 2020.* Retrieved from Corporate McDonalds: https://corporate.mcdonalds.com/content/dam/gwscorp/assets/investors/financial-information/annual-reports/2020%20Annual%20Report.pdf

Osterwalder, A., & Pigneur, Y. (2010). *Business Model Generation.* Chichester, England: John Wiley & Sons.

Sirkin, H. L., Keenan, P., & Jackson, A. (2005, October). *The Hard Side of Change Management.* Retrieved from Harvard Business Review: https://hbr.org/2005/10/the-hard-side-of-change-management

TNS, B. B. (2014). *State of Workplace Mental Health in Australia.* https://www.headsup.org.au/docs/default-source/

resources/bl1270-report---tns-the-state-of-mental-health-in-australian-workplaces-hr.pdf?sfvrsn=8.

Tschimmel, K. (2012). Design Thinking as an Effective Toolkit for Innovation. *Proceedings of the XXIII ISPIM Conference: Action for Innovation: Innovating from Experience.* Barcelona.

Ulrich, D., & Brockbank, W. (2005). *The HR Value Proposition.* Boston, MA: Harvard Business School Press.

Ulrich, D., Ulrich, M., Kryscynski, D., & Brockbank, W. (2017). *Victory Through Organization.* New York, NY: McGraw Hill Education.

Acknowledgements

We would like to acknowledge all those that have contributed to the research for this book, along with colleagues whose collaboration have helped shape our insights.

Thank you to:

Jeremy Andrulis, Faiz Buksh, Lisa Calderone, Sonya Clancy, Gerhard Diedericks, Kirsten Forgione, Natalie Herman, Ash Jurburg, Alex King, Kate Klease, Nathan Koukouras, Mary Markerink, Jordan Papadopoulos, Michael Pasqual, Darren Peiris, Radhika Peri, Anne Ridgeway, Belinda Ryan, Raj Tapper, and Damian Zahra.

Thank you to our network of Business Partners and clients for your participation in our forums and programs. Your support and input have been instrumental in shaping what we share with a broader audience in this book.

Rita Cincotta

To my family, Darren, Matthew, Siena and Noah, thanks for enabling me to do what I love every day. Your support, guidance, empathy and love fulfills me and nourishes my soul.

To my extended family and friends, thank you for your support, inspiration and love. Our village is generous and supportive and for that we are forever grateful.

George Liberopoulos

To my beautiful wife, Teresa. Thank you for all your support, inspiration and unconditional love. I am blessed to have you by my side.

To my amazing kids, Mia and James. You are my inspiration. Follow your passion and life's purpose. Dream big, do amazing things, and always do good. I love you.

Thank you to my inspiring parents. Mum and Dad, I'm blessed to have your patience, care, and unconditional love. Thank you to Teresa's mother, Concetta, for her love, selflessness and never-ending support.

To my extended family and friends – thank you. I'm blessed to have your assistance, guidance and love in my life.